Iron Man, Silken Heart
Bill Britt's Father Power

IRON MAN
SILKEN HEART
BILL BRITT'S FATHER POWER

Shivaram **Kumar**

Iron Man, Silken Heart
Bill Britt's Father Power
By Shivaram Kumar

Printed in the United States of America
ISBN: 978-0-692-56618-3

Published by Shivaram Kumar
www.MyWordsMyWorld.com

Learn more at
www.IronManSilkenHeart.com

For existing IBOs only. Not for use with prospects.
CR89584

Dedicated To
My Loving Family,
My Mentors,
&
The stubborn, passionate, and relentless dreamer
who does not know how to quit.

IRON MAN
SILKEN HEART
BILL BRITT'S FATHER POWER

Preamble:
An Exceptional Leader
In A Fascinating Business

In 1959, a small group of entrepreneurs laid the foundation for a unique business opportunity. This led to the formation of the Amway Corporation, headquartered in Ada, Michigan.

The company provides a low cost, low risk opportunity for anyone to start their own business. It is particularly attractive to people wanting to create extra income on a part-time basis, without jeopardizing their primary sources of income. With the right amount of time and effort, it can lead to financial opportunity, flexibility and freedom.

The Amway Sales and Marketing plan rewards its Independent Business Owners (IBOs) for selling products and helping other IBOs that they sponsor into the business, do the same.

Almost six decades after its inception, more than 3 million people worldwide are forging their own path to success. During this period, its compensation plan has paid out over 50 billion dollars to Independent Business Owners. Amway is family owned, and financially very stable. It is a global community, operating in more than 100 countries and territories.

The company initially offered a few exclusive cleaning products. As it grew into a more sophisticated business, the product lines expanded to the fields of health and beauty, their two most popular and profitable fields today. With the advent of the Internet, Amway became a significant player in e-commerce. It has also partnered, over time, with major name-brand companies.

Bill and Peggy Britt started their Amway business in Chapel Hill, North Carolina, in 1970, and today their network spans the globe. Their organization is massive, including over 1.5 million Independent Business Owners at its highest, and their influence in the Amway business is legendary.

Bill Britt dedicated the last 40 years of his life to developing his Amway business all over the world. His passion for the Amway business and the people in it was unwavering until the very end of his life. He and Peggy continued to invest their time and energy in the business, long after they no longer needed the income to sustain their enviable lifestyle, persevering in spite of Bill's prolonged health challenges. They grew one of the largest direct selling organizations in the history of the business.

Even though Bill Britt was a true leader in his own right, his life is inseparable from the story of Amway. For those who knew him and seek to emulate his brand of leadership and love for people, he made history through the Amway business.

The purpose of this book is to introduce Bill Britt to those who never had the chance to meet him, and to reveal that there are men of character who have made a difference in today's world in an untraditional manner. This book is not an infomercial about Amway or direct selling at large. It is a factual representation of how a visionary has impacted people all over the world in a positive way. This book is about Bill Britt's thought process and experiences. His consistency, wisdom, method of communication, clarity and openness can be useful lessons to all who care to listen, whether or not they are associated with the Amway business. So, whether you know it or not, you will want to know what Bill Britt knew. About people, about success, about courage, about principles, about laughing, loving and living.

Your success is measured by the number of people that are better off because you lived.

—Bill Britt

Iron Man, Silken Heart

The Never-Ending Eulogy

I started to write this book by first identifying the chapters and then adding parts to them as thoughts and memories came to me, based on experience, research and interviews with people who knew Bill Britt well. Bill was one of the world's greatest storytellers. For him, every story carried a message. Bill's choice of words was unique, and his delivery unforgettable. His words were rapid fire, energetic and often hilarious, and at the same time, very candid and forthright. I have attempted to organize each chapter the way he always taught – an anecdote or two from yesteryears followed by a powerful message.

Bill Britt passed away on January 23, 2013. While I have made changes to reflect this fact throughout the book, I have deliberately maintained the present tense in the first part of the chapter entitled "Enter Bill Britt."

Everyone who knew and loved Bill, feels his constant presence. For his wife Peggy, Bill has been the love of her life for more than 50 years. He led her into a world of dreams and together they created an exceptional and uncommon life. They never had children of their own, but their legacy will live on for generations. Their business family knows no geographical, linguistic, ethnic or religious boundaries, and today this family numbers in the millions. Even after Bill's passing, Peggy's life has revolved around Bill's larger-than-life presence and the empire he created. For those of us who have had the great opportunity to sit at Bill's feet and learn from him for more than two decades, we feel his presence in the way we live our lives, the words that we speak, the people we associate and grow with, and those times we laugh together.

Britt Worldwide is a training system founded by Bill Britt and the leaders on his team. It is independent of Amway, but approved and accredited by it. In essence, it is a training system that enables Independent Business Owners powered by Amway to work with marketing, sales and leadership development.

Bill's legacy is being managed by the Management Operating Committee of Britt Worldwide LLC. This committee consists of Paul Miller, Angelo Nardone, Kanti Gala, Raj Shah and myself. If each of our lives were to be a line, the intersection of those lines would be Bill Britt. We know each other because of Bill Britt. He is the common factor. When we meet, our unspoken mantra is "WWBBD: What Would Bill Britt Do?" as we make decisions that affect many lives around the world.

For the community of Independent Business Owners worldwide, Bill Britt continues to live through his teachings. His classic talks like "Father Power," "Cast In Concrete," "It is the Size of the Fight in the Dog," "Power of Words" and "Self-Image and Attitude" play every day on thousands of CD players and streaming devices all over the globe. Hundreds of conferences with thousands of attendees see him on big screens throughout the year. The Britt Worldwide (BWW) system is one of the most successful business systems in the world. Originally designed to support Amway Independent Business Owners, its core teachings are applicable to any walk of life. Today, many corporations and educational institutions are interested in adopting the methods of BWW to improve their productivity and effectiveness.

When Bill Britt started to build his business in 1970, I was a small boy in elementary school in India. Two decades later, in the 90s, I became part of his business team. As I became more deeply involved, I realized that Bill's teachings had been consistent from the very beginning. I had access to recordings of his talks from the early 70s. I was able to confirm his consistency over the years by comparing what he was teaching in the 1970s to what I was hearing in the 1990s and beyond. His teachings were steady as a rock, and many of his predictions had come true. Today there are people in their early twenties succeeding well in my business team who hadn't even been born when I got involved. They have access to the latest recordings of all the talks and videos by BWW leaders, and they have technology that was not even a dream in the 80s and early 90s. But still, what inspires them most are talks by Bill Britt, made during the 70s, 80s, and 90s, and all the way to

2012. It is therefore more than reasonable to assume that kids yet unborn will be influenced by Bill Britt, and for many, many, many generations to come.

In that sense, Bill Britt lives. He will continue to live. The values and principles he taught are time-tested and evergreen. There is a little Bill Britt in everyone who has been influenced by him. Very few people have had the kind of impact that Bill Britt has had on millions of people around the world.

Every eulogy is special. Words and stories are chosen carefully and shared with a lot of emotion. The truth, however, is that most eulogies are short-lived. All too often, sadly enough, a eulogy is the only time someone is talked about in a positive light for any length of time.

Bill Britt's eulogy was simply a natural extension of the respect and praise that people have always had for him, and will continue to have. Bill's influence is so great that people will never stop talking about him. This eulogy will never end.

So, Bill Britt lives. In our hearts and minds. In our thought process, our decisions. In the way we love, live and give. Bill Britt lives in the way we teach, work and laugh. He really does.

Iron Man, Silken Heart

Gratitude & Latitude

Gratitude

I have always wanted to write a book. When I was in eighth grade I wrote detective novels, but only a few people ever saw them. They were hand-written in regular ruled notebooks. For decades now I have often thought about writing a book. Many people encouraged me, but life took me in many other exciting directions. Now I know that there was a master plan in action. Life was preparing me for this special opportunity. My first book had to be about the person who has impacted my life in a unique way, and shown me possibilities that I did not know existed. For that, I am grateful.

My parents, thank you for encouraging me to become a voracious reader, immersing me in a world of books, and believing that I could achieve anything I set my mind to. Your hard work and sacrifices paved the way for an incredible journey which ultimately led me to the inner circle of many amazing individuals like Bill Britt and his leadership team.

My Anjali, thank you for 23 glorious years of marriage, and your constant support throughout our journey together as entrepreneurs. Thank you for always staying calm and positive, and your unconditional support in every endeavor of mine. I have ventured into many unknown areas, sometimes without success, but you never criticized me or questioned my judgment. This is my first attempt at writing a book, but you never doubted whether I would come through. I believe there are two reasons for this: one, you believe in me 100%, and two, you knew that I had a special connection with Bill Britt, and that my heart was yearning to tell his story.

My daughters Devika, Tarika and Ritika, thank you for giving up a big part of our usual travels and outings and helping me get organized. Thank you for keeping track of the things I would remember about Uncle Bill while driving in the car with you. Devika, thank you for going through the book in great detail. You helped eliminate redundancies and clarify ambiguities to make my endeavor to encapsulate Uncle Bill the best it could be.

My parents-in-law, who have been two of the strongest cheerleaders in our lives, in recent years. They have been encouraging me to write a book for many years now. As I worked on this book, my father-in-law would constantly nudge me to "get it done quickly."

Peggy Britt, you are amazing. You were the center of Bill's universe, just as he was yours. Your unconditional support of Bill is an inspiration to thousands of couples around the world. Thank you for traveling countless miles with Bill by road and air to share and give to so many thousands of people. Thank you for all that you have done, and continue to do for the BWW organization. Thank you for giving me the valuable input that made this book possible.

Rich DeVos and Jay Van Andel, you founded the Amway Corporation. You started a ripple effect that is never ending. Even the greatest leaders in the world need a role model, someone they can look up to. Bill Britt had a deep-rooted respect for your vision, integrity and tenacity.

Doug DeVos and Steve Van Andel, thank you for keeping the dream alive and blazing. Bill often gloated over how he enjoyed the privilege of watching you blossom into the leaders that you are today. He was proud of how you have taken the batons from your fathers and continue to raise Amway to greater heights around the globe. Special thanks to the two of you for going the extra mile for this book. You took time out of your schedules and carved out the space to talk about Bill. You didn't just send me quotes, you sent me the script of a dialog you shared about Bill Britt, specifically for this book. I cannot thank you enough.

Victors, Hansens, Yagers, you are the dream givers. Bill had nothing but admiration and love for you. Meeting Dexter changed Bill and Peggy's lives forever, and through them, millions of other lives were impacted. Dex, you were his hero.

Paul Miller, Angelo Nardone, Kanti Gala and Raj Shah, thank you for serving the BWW team. I am honored to be able to share the responsibility of the

BWW Management Operating Committee with all of you. Thank you for sharing the stories and experiences I have included in this book.

The members of the Independent Business Owners Association International, Inc. (IBOAI), thank you for being the voice of hundreds of thousands of entrepreneurs. Your predecessors were instrumental in establishing the foundational principles upon which the Amway Corporation was built, and to this day, you carry forth your responsibilities in a manner consistent with those principles.

Claudia Nardone, you were the first one to go through my first draft in great detail. Your input was insightful, and it really helped bring out the human element inside of the Superman named Bill Britt.

BWW LLC members and BWW Diamonds, hats off to you! You are the leaders of Bill Britt's legacy. You are keeping Bill's dream alive and are the reason his teachings will reach people yet to be born. Without your stories and experiences, this book would have been incomplete. Your overwhelming love for Bill and Peggy is obvious. I often got teary-eyed while reading your emails about them and how much they have impacted all our lives.

Manipal and Renuka Reddy, Sudheer and Sulbha Solapurkar, Pravin and Madhu Chheda, Kanti and Lata Gala, thank you for leading me to this wonderful business opportunity and into Bill Britt's inner circle.

Lisa Madison, CEO of BWW, and the entire BWW staff, thank you for helping me through the process of making this book a reality. It would not have been possible if not for your hard work and dedication to both Bill Britt and this book. Thank you, Chuck Newman, for sifting through piles of old photos of Bill and fine-tuning the presentation.

Achala Upendran, thank you for your help with the editing process. You meticulously corrected grammatical errors and simplified the formatting to organize my ideas best.

Latitude

Bill Britt had an inimitable style. Most of his teachings were off the cuff and spontaneous. His talks usually had a central theme that he developed on, and he would weave through them real life experiences, funny anecdotes and powerful messages. His thoughts and experiences have never been captured in writing, until now. A good portion of my material comes from Bill's stage talks, which have shaped my life for over two decades. However, I have also had the privilege of spending a considerable amount of time with Bill off-stage. Even though he was the same person in private as he was in public, there was something special about spending time with him in his home, watching him walk the dog, listening to him sing and play the piano, witnessing him get upset at the roof guy, laughing at jokes, seeing him relate to kids and adults alike, and sitting at his feet, learning. I believe these interactions were crucial in my endeavor to tell Bill's story, to best capture his idiosyncrasies, values, and unparalleled zest for life and learning.

Packaging Bill Britt in a book is a daunting task, because he was gifted in so many uncommon ways. His knowledge was extremely diverse. He was able to relate to anyone and everyone, no matter their race, ethnicity, age or profession. His talks were multi-dimensional, peppered with subtle comments, humor, and often controversial, even outrageous punch lines. So I have taken the liberty of employing a little latitude while writing this book. Not all of his quotes have been reproduced verbatim. I have paraphrased and made adjustments where appropriate for reasons of brevity and presentation. At the same time, I have worked hard to preserve the essence of his style and personality.

Bill's talks were rapid-fire, and he punctuated serious messages with captivating and often funny stories. For instance, he spoke frequently about the three powers: the power of the spoken word, the power of unity, and the power of submission. Typically, he would not cover these in one straight stretch. He would cover one of the powers, segue into a related topic, and then discuss the next power. I have tried to maintain a similar flow in this book by dividing these powers into separate chapters.

For those of you who may be unfamiliar with the Amway business, terms like Platinum, Ruby, Emerald, Diamond, Executive Diamond, Double Diamond, Triple Diamond, Crown and Crown Ambassador are levels of achievement in the Amway business. They broadly represent increasing levels of achievement and income. The only way to reach these levels is to help other people succeed. Bill and Peggy Britt reached the Crown level in both North America and India. The significance of this is that countless lives have been better off because they built the Amway business.

I have frequently referred to the Britts' lifestyle. Their Amway income has always been substantial. In addition, they also derived income from Britt Worldwide, just as other leaders do, in the form of speaking fees and compensation from tools such as CDs and books. I have used the term "the business" to include both Amway and Britt Worldwide incomes and activities.

I have often used the term "financially free" to describe someone who has built a successful Amway business. In the context of this book, this refers to an income level that has enabled the individual or couple to depart from a routine job to make a living. These are people who are making or have made "ongoing" income through the business that allowed them to "retire" from a traditional 9 to 5 way of making a living, and devote themselves to their own business full-time.

I have taken care to give proper credit to people while using their quotes. Quotes that do not have a name attached to them are mine.

While including stories that the great people of the BWW organization have shared with me, I have given priority to uniqueness or relevance rather than seniority or level of achievement in the business. Even though each person's experience is special, I have attempted to avoid repetition and redundancy. I have also included a chapter entitled "Homage" to include many of the noteworthy comments and stories I received from leaders in Britt Worldwide.

I have added a "Chapter Captures" section at the end of each chapter except for the ones entitled "Enter Bill Britt" and "Enter Bill Britt II". In this section, I have listed the salient points of each chapter.

I pray that you are not able to put this book down until you finish reading it. That is the way a book about Bill Britt ought to be.

Enter Bill Britt

A jam-packed coliseum. Over 15,000 people in attendance. There would have been 30,000 or more, space permitting. It could be in Richmond, Knoxville, Spokane, Shanghai, Chennai, India or Warsaw, Poland. This could be at any time during the 70s, 80s or 90s, or the first decade of the millennium. The excitement is thick in the air, and the energy of anticipation is unmistakable. Judging by the possible locations and years, this could not be the Super Bowl, the Olympics, a Hollywood event or a political gathering. Strangely, for an event of this magnitude, what is missing is the press. No paparazzi, no annoying reporters. So you know this is not an audience that has gathered to listen to the President of the United States or the Queen of England. If this is China or India, many people have traveled three days by train or on foot and have overcome significant challenges to attend this event. Not all of them can afford the FM radio that is required for them to be able to listen to their favorite speaker translated into their own languages. Those who can, know that the translator can only convey the words, but not the essence of what the speaker has to say. The listeners don't care, because their connection with the speaker transcends words. It is a unique, unusual connection. This speaker is not a flash in the pan entertainer. He is not a typical motivational speaker who is here now and gone the next minute, with no promise of continuity or meaningful mentorship. More importantly, he is not just a speaker. He is a doer.

It is time. The stage lights are up. The music is unmistakable. It is either "Eye of the Tiger" from Rocky or "I Feel Good" by James Brown. There is a huge but simple logo that says "BWW - Empowering People Around the World" that serves as a backdrop. There are huge video screens so everyone in the coliseum can see the speaker's expressions and his eyes. The people in the front are there because they spent a good part of the previous night waiting in line, paying little heed to sleep or food. There are no teleprompters, slide shows, or even a podium. Chances are that the speaker will not use any notes.

The host of the evening comes up, trembling with excitement, immensely grateful for the opportunity to introduce the speaker. Typically the host of the event has been able to create a lot of success in his personal, financial and spiritual life because of this special person. He is one of thousands around the world who has benefited from knowing this man. This is a very special moment for the host.

The crowd is ecstatic. They cheer and shout like they never will for a movie star, politician or religious leader. This is where they shed their inhibitions and become kids. Look, there they are, fully grown adults screaming with excitement, standing on their chairs like teenagers at a rock concert. But instead of infatuation, their emotions range from gratitude to admiration to belief...in themselves and their own dreams.

Enter Bill Britt.

Living the Quotes

Bill Britt, one of the greatest teachers of this century, one of the biggest hope-givers ever known to humankind.

Bill Britt, one of the most consistent human beings ever. Arguably one of the most photographed public figures. One of the most admired people in the world.

Bill Britt was someone you could count on. He was the bulldog you would have wanted in your corner if you were in a fight. He was the teddy bear you needed when you were discouraged or challenged.

What differentiated Bill Britt from other people of influence such as authors and motivational speakers, preachers and politicians is the continuity of his connection with people. He did not simply espouse beliefs without providing a vehicle for people to successfully implement them. His students get to listen to him on an ongoing basis, with concrete steps that they can take to fulfill their dreams and goals. Anyone can attend a weekend seminar on success, but they may not always find it easy to translate what they learn into their everyday lives…unless they are part of an organization like Britt Worldwide.

Bill Britt taught, provided a concrete vehicle, and followed through with an army of leaders that he helped develop all over the world.

The vehicle that Bill Britt has used is, primarily, the well-known Amway business. The world recognizes Amway as a pioneer in direct selling, offering high quality products in nutrition, skin care, and home care. In 2015, Amway and parent company Alticor reached a global sales figure of $9.5 billion. When Bill and his wife Peggy started their Amway business back in 1970, it was a 12-year-old company, doing just $120 million in sales. Stalwart business leaders like Bill and Peggy Britt played a major role in the meteoric rise of the company, raising it to its current dizzying heights. In this manner, not only were they able to achieve an uncommon level of freedom and lifestyle for themselves, but they were also able to help others do the same.

Simply put, the Amway model allows people to start their own business and build a team of business owners to move products manufactured by Amway and its affiliates into the marketplace. Most people outside of the business only have a vague idea of what that entails. As long as the laws of the land are not violated, and certain rules adhered to, Amway empowers people to build the business using their own individual styles and methods. Many people think of their team as a "sales force" alone, and drive their business in that direction. However, Bill Britt's style was to develop and empower leaders, and give them the same opportunity he had. He has done this very successfully all over the world.

> *Many people use people to build their business. I believe that you should use the business to build people.*
>
> *—Bill Britt*

Bill Britt could hardly appear in public without being recognized. Every time he spoke, someone would always have a recording device in his face because he was always sharing his knowledge and experiences. You could always learn a life lesson from Bill. You would remember the lesson for sure, and you would never forget his choice of words and his delivery.

Bill was a dreamer and an overcomer. His determination and grit were of legendary proportions. He was very strongly opinionated, yet non-judgmental.

Peggy Britt, Bill's first and only wife of 50 years, has supported him steadfastly. She was always by his side through thick and thin. Together, they lived a great life. They bought several properties, and Bill acquired a collection of more than 55 cars, several airplanes including a Falcon 50 jet, and multiple helicopters. They spent a good amount of their time entertaining family and people in their business. They often refer to their Amway team as their family. It is not often that you see the kind of long-lasting relationships of love and loyalty that this couple has developed all over the world.

There is no dearth of quotable quotes in this world. Speakers often use metaphors, alliterations and impactful words to make their points. Here are a few examples:

If you help enough people get what they want, you can get what you want.

—Zig Ziglar

People don't care how much you know until they know how much you care.

—John Maxwell

Do unto others as you would have them do unto you.

—The Golden Rule

Don't just talk the talk. You must also walk the walk.

—Unknown

Delivering quotes is one thing. Living them is a whole different story. Bill Britt lived these and other quotes day in and day out. Having been under his mentorship, thousands of people around the world now do the same.

You will find children in rural India and China quoting Bill Britt. There are couples in England, Australia, South Africa, Thailand and many other countries who will testify that they owe their strong marriages to Bill's teachings. You will find people treasuring the one picture they were able to get with Bill and Peggy. In remote villages around the world, you will see those pictures hanging in the most prominent places in people's homes. When he visited the Taj Mahal in India, the tour guides were taken aback by the overwhelming number of people who wanted a picture taken with him. They commented that even the Queen of England had not received the kind of attention that Bill Britt commanded.

Bill Britt was an authority on network marketing, or multi-level marketing.

You may not be aware of how legitimate multi-level companies really work, but that should only inspire you to want to learn. For now, it should suffice for you to know that a multi-level business, when built properly, is one of the most fascinating, challenging and fulfilling exercises in team building, leadership development and relationship management in the history of the world. If Bill Britt was able to lead engineers, farmers, scientists, lawyers, doctors, housewives and students around the world to a better economic future and way of living, then common sense dictates that there has to be something special about him and the Amway business. In fact, the truth is that there is something more than special about this business. It teaches life lessons like no other business can. Any organization consisting of people, be it a family or a large corporation, can benefit from Bill Britt's unique teachings.

> *An authority on multi-level marketing is an authority on relationships, leadership and team building. Without question.*

Bill Britt always believed that the dreamer never stops dreaming. He knew that on the day he died, he would leave some unfulfilled dreams behind. In Bill's case, one of his visions that has yet to come true was his desire to take his teachings to people who were not in his sphere of influence. He wanted the world to learn about the simple but unique principles he taught and lived by. Another vision was to break a hundred new Diamonds in BWW in one single year.

The BWW Management Operating Committee (MOC) is committed to seeing these visions come true. This book is a step in that direction.

I would like to repeat what I wrote earlier –

> *Whether you know this or not, you want to know what Bill knew. About people, about success, about courage, about principles, about laughing, loving and living.*

Bill & Peggy welcomed onstage at a business conference in the 1970s (above) and in the 1990s. Over the course of four decades, the Britts spoke to over a million business owners at events around the world.

Bill & Peggy celebrating Free Enterprise Day.

> *You cannot be personally free unless you are economically free.*
>
> *—Bill Britt*

The Why:
The Power of Dreams
& Written Goals

Bill used all of life's experiences to propel him into a bigger and better future. He developed the traits of a dreamer, traits that he would use to change the world. Even though he did not always do so consciously, he was constantly preparing for success.

As a young, responsible son of an alcoholic father, Bill had to work hard to support his mother and the rest of the family. He never kept any of the money he earned from working at the grocery store or the newspaper route for himself. He gave all of it to his mother, and kept this up until the age of 23. This included the time he served in the military in Korea. When he returned, his father presented him with a new Buick, which was totally financed. Bill had to make the payments. His parents had not kept aside for him any of the money he had sent to them. He had to start from scratch.

Bill's tough childhood could have made him a bitter person. Instead, he made lemonade from the lemons that life had thrown at him. The root of his childhood problems was his father's alcoholism. So for his part, Bill decided to stay away from alcohol. In fact, he taught people not to mix alcohol with business meetings. Even today, BWW strongly recommends against the use of alcohol in any business-building event, be it in a home or in a coliseum. We organize major conferences in different cities around the world, and are probably one of the largest users of hotel rooms as businesses go, but hardly any alcohol is bought or consumed at these hotels and meeting venues.

While in Korea, Bill was recognized for his great attitude and positive outlook. He only had good things to say about his time in the military. He would talk about how great the food was, and how much he appreciated the opportunity to serve his country. Bill was clearly leadership material even then, since he went in as a private and came out as an officer ("in no time," as he would say).

Indeed, Bill's patriotism was deep-rooted. His dreams were shaped by the love he bore for his country. This would become evident in the way he conducted his life and, later on, his business. Today, every major conference organized by the BWW system starts off with the Pledge of Allegiance. We have a yearly weekend conference named "Free Enterprise Days" where we celebrate the freedoms that make America the great country that it is. One prominent feature of this event is that there is special recognition for anyone who has served in the armed forces. We also have a special presentation of the Color Guard. This has been a practice for over four decades and is an integral part of the Britt legacy.

The Journey Back Home

Write down your vision upon tablets.

—Habakkuk 2:2

Upon his return from Korea, Bill found himself on a train to South Carolina from Washington State. It was a five-day journey and he did not have much to do. His eyes fell upon a skinny book on how to have a dream and develop a vision. So he picked it up and read it. On the last page, the author had provided some space for the reader to write their top five goals. This is what Bill wrote:

1. *Marry a beautiful woman (a beauty title holder)*
2. *Make $10,000 by the time I am 30 years old*
3. *Retire at the age of 40*
4. *Be successful in my own business*
5. *Become a millionaire*

As it turned out, each and every one of these goals came true.

Marry a beautiful woman

Bill met Peggy in September 1956. The moment he laid eyes on her, he knew she was the one. She held a beauty title – the Dairy Princess of North Carolina. They were married on July 13, 1957. She was beautiful not just on the outside, but on the inside as well. She was to become his strength. She supported him through thick and thin and never questioned him. Her life revolved around him and his needs. He would explain to others that she was in total submission to him, and he was in total submission to her. They were very much in love with each other and set a great example for thousands of couples around the world.

Peggy's simplicity and beauty always shines through her words and actions. Her homes are always perfect, with everything from the furniture to the flowers coordinated artistically. She has always been a gracious host. Every time I stayed with the Britts, I was treated with unconditional love.

To see Bill and Peggy do things together was like watching a symphony of two. Even when they fussed at each other, it was just as perfect as when they would compliment each other.

In 1967, before they started their successful Amway business, Bill borrowed $10,000 from a bank to invest in a deal that turned out to be fraudulent. To put this in perspective, using 4.1% as the inflation rate, $10,000 back then translates to roughly $72,000 in 2016. However, Peggy never criticized or condemned him. She stood strong by his side and assured him that she would continue to work at her job and contribute towards the bank payment each month. She had faith in her man, and that increased Bill's respect for her and motivated him to do bigger and better things to give her the best life possible.

Make $10,000 by the time I am 30 years old

Bill was trained as an engineer and worked his way up to becoming an Assistant to the City Manager of Raleigh, North Carolina, and was eventually designated the City Manager of Sanford, North Carolina. His annual salary was $10,000. He was 30 years old. Bill credited his rapid career growth to his work ethic and willingness to go the extra mile. He developed these traits under the influence of his maternal grandfather as he worked in the farms during summers in La Grange, North Carolina as a child.

Retire at the age of 40

Bill saw the Amway business at the age of 38, and became financially free at the age of 40. He quit his job as City Manager on July 4, 1972. In the conventional sense, retirement implies "pulling back" or "slowing down" and leading a quiet life. To Bill Britt and the people he mentored, retirement meant freedom from being controlled by money. It meant living to the fullest, being productive and busying oneself helping others achieve the same level of freedom.

Be successful in my own business and become a millionaire

It cost Bill and Peggy $21 to get started in their own Amway business in 1970. From that humble beginning, they have built a gigantic business empire that spans the globe. They have received a multi-million dollar income from their Amway business each year for several decades now. That would likely not be the case in a traditional business, or if Bill had still been a City Manager somewhere.

All the goals that Bill wrote down in that little book came true in exactly the way he had written them.

Bill encouraged people to write down their goals. "There is magic in written goals," he would often say. He would patiently sit down with anyone who needed help, and teach them how to put down goals in every aspect of their life – spiritual, health, relationships, wealth, lifestyle, and so on – on paper. Many Independent Business Owners, including my wife and I, are fanatical about our belief in the power of written goals. We cannot claim that every goal that we have written down has come true exactly, but by and large, we have seen the magic work in our lives.

Financial Security

Out of Bill's five written goals, four had to do with money and financial security. The lack of money during his formative years made Bill realize how important it was to be economically secure. After serving in the army, the G.I. Bill allowed him to go to college, where he pursued his masters in civil engineering. His experience in the army and his ability as a natural leader took him through a course of events that led to his becoming the City Manager of the city of Sanford in North

Carolina. By then he was married to Peggy, who worked as an office secretary.

Bill worked hard and had a full plate. While he was both a City Manager and a graduate student, Bill also ran a National Guard unit. He and Peggy enjoyed a good marriage, a nice house, and status in society. Bill had realized his goal of making $10,000 by the age of 30. He "looked good and smelled good," but in his own words, he was broke. He was a dedicated City Manager for 15 years, but was woefully aware of the fact that he was not in charge of his own life.

Outwardly, he looked good. No city employee made more money than he did. He was the Big Kahuna. He was the big boss, but he had bosses, too. He had no control over actions beyond his pay grade, actions that could affect his job. He had no control over who got elected to the city council. He had been through some bad experiences in those areas. He developed a strong desire to create additional income to try and protect his and Peggy's future. Every Sunday, he would check the newspaper and circle in red any business opportunity. He had bought a Mooney 21 aircraft that he would fly to different places to check out business opportunities. He looked into baby shoes, rubber stamps, car washes, corner launderettes, hamburgers and even Dunkin' Donuts.

"You cannot be personally free unless you are economically free."
—*Bill Britt*

Bill believed that economic freedom and personal freedom were like conjoined twins. You couldn't have one without the other. He realized that as long as someone else was signing his paycheck, he was not economically free.

Economic freedom became Bill Britt's first big dream. He would often say that he got into Amway for five reasons – money, money, money, money and money! It was not that money was the most important thing in the world. The real message was that if he did not control money, then money would automatically control him. That meant he could never be personally free. Bill's goal was to make so much money that it became a non-issue in his life, and he could concentrate on helping others succeed. When he could get to a point where he was not spending all his time chasing the almighty dollar bill, he could devote himself to learning and teaching others about the things that really mattered, such as health, freedom, relationships, faith and love.

And that is exactly what he did, with Peggy by his side, for more than four decades.

The catalysts that helped Bill's dreams turn into reality were his attitude, faith, optimism, tenacity, love for his country and love for people. His dreams evolved from personal freedom to making a difference in other people's lives. The nature of the Amway business is that it provides an uncommon degree of control and freedom to those who build it the proper way. It is not a utopia, but for those who can make it work, it comes pretty close. It is not fraught with glass ceilings, politics and prejudices that may be considered typical in other, more traditional businesses. People who are successful in the Amway business generally tend to be light-hearted and cheerful, and the fact that they are not bogged down with the daily drudgery of chasing the buck definitely shows in their way of life.

Bill used his freedom to help other people become free. He gave his time to others to help them believe in themselves and in the free enterprise system. He would unashamedly share his opinions with others, and did not hide the fact that he was a conservative Christian. He was able to share from his heart and tell people exactly where he stood, because he was not anyone's puppet.

In my opinion, the irony in America today is that freedom of speech decreases as a person's influence increases. Many politicians cannot speak their minds because of political correctness, or reluctance to offend certain organizations. Billionaire businessmen often choose to be careful with their words so as not to attract the ire of the media or the IRS. We hear of many articulate preachers, but their words are sometimes biased, measured and calculating. Hollywood stars who dare to express conservative views get beaten up by the media. Speeches are carefully scripted, and teleprompters employed.

Bill Britt was the first public figure I saw who spoke from his heart. That is why his talks were so refreshing. He did not have any agenda because he was his own man. He was not controlled by a political party or an invisible Board of Directors, hovering somewhere in the background.

When someone speaks from their heart with unconditional love for people, you respect, enjoy and cherish them, even if you don't always agree with them.

A big dreamer always has a great following. When communicating his vision, Bill had a wide range of people in his audience. He knew that the overwhelming problem for most of his newer listeners had to do with lack of money. So he would draw them in by telling them his story of how true financial freedom was possible in the Amway business. He would talk about things that people could relate to, like owning a house and a nice car. He would speak of getting and staying out of debt. This dream-building process would go on, from jewelry to wardrobes to world travel to private yachts and planes. He would stretch people's imaginations. Then he would move on to address his more mature audiences and talk about the foundation of America and the free enterprise system. He would urge people to dream big and make those dreams come true. In his opinion, that was how we could make the world a better place to live in. He constantly pushed people to find out what their "why" was.

"You need a big reason, a big dream. The dream gives you your 'why.' The bigger your dream, the bigger your 'why.' All you need is a body temperature, your dream and some guts. The 'how' don't amount to a hill of beans unless you know 'why.'"

"My why is I want a free country to live in — that means people who are truly free. That means they control their government and not the other way around. You need your freedom to be the person you want to be."

"My freedom will have more meaning when every man and woman by my side is free not just physically, but psychologically."

"We want you to be guilty of unleashing the goodness of many hearts and many minds."

"I have another simple dream: to develop some manhood in America. Too many men today are sitting and doing nothing but wearing the hair off the back of their heads watching the idiot box and drinking beer. We need more dreamers. There is no lack of people to fulfill dreams. There is only a lack of dreamers. Find your 'why,' be a dreamer."

— Excerpts from Bill's talk entitled "The Why."

Chapter Captures

- The "why" is more important than the "how." Success begins with a dream.

- A dream with a date becomes a goal.

- Something magical happens when we write down our goals.

Bill & Peggy cut the cake at their wedding reception on July 13, 1957.

Bill receiving a medal for service during the Korean War.

Bill & Peggy: the young Army officer with his beauty queen.

Bill in one of his first postings as a city manager in North Carolina.

> *Show me how a person lives today and I will show you the words they used in the past. Show me how a person speaks today and I will show you how they will live in the future.*
>
> *—Bill Britt*

Seeds:
The Power of Words

"I can't help thinking about a kid who wanted his own pony. But his dad was an alcoholic and always had a money problem. I can't help but see the kid with tears in his eyes. He was too embarrassed to bring his friends home because of his father. But the kid said, someday I will show him. I will do whatever it takes. One day I will have a pony of my own. My ship will come in for sure."

—Bill Britt

Bill was the oldest of eight kids, and started to work at the age of eleven. His father was a good man, but got involved with the wrong people and started to drink. Bill would often recall how the alcohol would transform his father into an abusive and violent person. His mother became very unhappy. She never knew what to expect when her husband came home. Bill's main motivation became to keep his mother, Vivian Britt, as happy as he could.

Vivian was a very talented piano player. At that tender age of eleven, Bill had the maturity to figure out that a piano in the house would give her an outlet, an escape from her constant worry and anxiety. While walking through the streets downtown, Bill often passed a piano store. One day, his eyes fell upon a good-looking Gulbransen piano, with a price tag of $565. He took his mother to the store and declared that he was going to buy the piano for her. Bill recalled this as his first significant dream.

Vivian told him that the family wouldn't be able to afford the piano, but Bill was always thinking of solutions. He knew he was too young to be able to earn a salary, but he could work for tips. He started his first job at A&P, bagging groceries. By the time he had turned twelve, Bill had added two paper routes to his job at the supermarket. He convinced his mother to sign up for an installment plan for the piano and used his income to make timely payments each month over three years. Once the Gulbransen was paid for, Bill turned all his income over to his mother to help support the family and raise the other children. He would tell us repeatedly that it was well worth it just to see the joy that the piano brought into his mother's life and into the lives of all the others who enjoyed her music.

"I am grateful that even before I became a teenager I had the maturity to figure out what would bring some much-needed joy into my mother's life. I decided to get her the piano, and then somehow figured out a way to pay for it. Not sure how many eleven-year-olds would do that."

—Bill Britt

At school, Bill was averaging Cs because he was working all the time. He did not have the luxury of a normal teenage life. During this period, his self-esteem was very low. He did not have many friends. He needed money, and he needed support. But most importantly, unbeknownst to him, he needed words of encouragement. He recalled two instances in his youth where words made all the difference. Later on in his life, Bill would carry the message of the power of words to the world.

The first instance was when his grandfather was on his deathbed. Bill and his mother were visiting him, and Bill's Uncle Harry was standing by the bed. Toward the end of the visit, Uncle Harry turned to Bill's mother and said, "Vivian, you have a sharp kid there. He has bright eyes and he is going to do something great with his life." From that point on, Harry became Bill's favorite relative. Those words were seeds planted in young Bill's heart.

The second instance was when Bill joined the army. An officer named Captain Schwartz invited Bill into his office and told him that he was impressed with his attitude and that he was officer material. Until that point, he and another cadet had been flunking their officer training class. But those words from the captain motivated the two of them to work together harder than ever before and as it turned out, harder than most others. They were the only two guys in the batch that had not gone to college. Bill recalled that out of 63 students, only 23 made the cut. He and his friend graduated number one and number two in the class.

Years later, Bill had learned and understood so much about the power of words that one of his primary messages was that spoken words can either create or destroy. The Bible corroborated his belief that words are powerful.

"Thou art snared by the words of thy mouth."
—*Proverbs 6:2, one of Bill's favorite verses from the Bible.*

Many, many books have been written about positive affirmation. The power of words has been taught by motivational speakers time and again. But no one taught it like Bill did.

Meet Verne

This is Verne, Bill's stick-man. Verne represents humanity. Bill used Verne to teach others about the power of words.

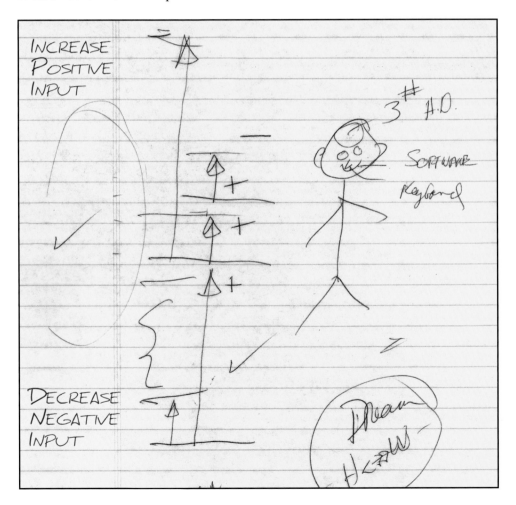

In Bill's words (paraphrased below):

This is Verne, the stick man. As you can see, he has two eyes, two ears, a mouth, and a nose. And the little blob in his head is his brain. This is what we are all about. The brain. Everything we believe and have ever heard or recorded is stored in this 3-pound deal called the brain. All this information does not reside in Verne's elbow or knee. It's all in the brain. His beliefs, his thoughts, good or bad, true or false — they all reside in his brain.

The arrow with the plus sign next to it represents the positive and uplifting information in Verne's brain about himself and the world in general. The arrow with the minus sign next to it represents the negative information. If Verne has more negative than positive information in his brain, he has a net negative self-image, which is the case with most people who did not have a positive upbringing or simply grow up just watching news and talk shows or have been subjecting themselves to gossip and negative company. The negative far exceeds the positive. Now what do we do? You can't delete files in your brain like you do in a computer. Trying to forget something is not a good way to forget something.

"The problem with trying to forget something is that you have to first remember that which you are trying to forget."

—*Bill Britt*

While you cannot delete the negatives in your brain, you can most certainly dilute them. If Verne caps the negative by staying away from situations and people that add negative to his brain, and instead develops a habit of reading positive books, listening to uplifting words, and associating with people who will encourage and edify him, he begins to dilute the negative in his brain with positive information. The negative is still there, but so diluted that it does not have the potency it once did.

A spoon of cyanide can kill you instantly. But when diluted with several gallons of water, it may only make you sick. There is a big difference between being sick and being dead.

—*Bill Britt*

Bill used Verne to teach people the importance of programming the brain for success and prosperity. Then he would point out to his audience that one of the most effective ways to program the brain was self-talk. He would explain that the words we speak to ourselves go back into our brain through our inner ear. They, like words from others, can either add to the plus side or the minus side. While we may not be able to control what others say, we have total control over what we say when we speak. People don't make a big deal of speaking words of self-defeat on a constant basis ("I am not good when it comes to time management," "I always seem to attract the wrong kind of people into my life," "I am a loser"). Bill would caution his students that these words could create lethal beliefs in our brains if we spoke them. He would ask us to say what we wanted, not what we have that we may not want ("I am getting better at time management," "I attract the very best in my life," "I am a winner").

There is no real measure of how much we have learned from Bill Britt. His most prominent message has had to do with the power of the spoken word. While speaking to an audience, be it just a few people or a full coliseum, it was typical of Bill to bring a new person up on stage and ask them questions about themselves, about their expectations and vision for the future. Normally, a new person would be tentative and vague with his or her answers. Then Bill would hold the microphone for the new person to speak, whisper words into their ear, and have them repeat these words aloud into the mic. They would be words of conviction, excitement and confidence. The audience would burst into spontaneous cheering and applause. Bill would then point out that he never asked anyone to cheer and applaud, but the words coming out of the new person's mouth inspired them to do so. The person was the same, but the words were different.

You Get What You Speak

Just around the time he started his Amway business in the 70s, Paul Miller (now a Crown IBO) was working for Peggy Britt as a product boy for $3 an hour. One day, as Bill walked by, Paul said "Mr. Britt, I can't get anybody into my business." "I know," replied Bill, as he kept walking. "You get what you speak."

During a function once, Bill started out with a really bad sore throat. He had the whole weekend ahead of him. On Friday night, his voice was down to a whisper, and people began to wonder if his voice would last until Sunday afternoon. Bill demonstrated the power of words to his audience: "Call on that which isn't as if it were, and it will be." He claimed that his voice would get better as the weekend progressed. Lo and behold, by Saturday evening he was sounding like his good old normal self.

Bill walked the talk. He lived by example and did not hesitate to remind people that their lives were a reflection of their words. Paul learned his lesson and went on to build one of the most successful businesses in the world of Amway. Today, Paul Miller is one of the most effective teachers of the power of the spoken word.

Bill Britt created a success system in the context of multi-level marketing, but applicable in all of business, which was founded on his belief in the power of words. The system consists of available audio and video recordings, weekend conferences, books, and team-building principles. In the end, these are all words that help people prepare for success and propel into action. Words that empower people to succeed and prosper in all the important areas of life.

The truth of the matter is that it is easy to validate all of this. At one end of the spectrum are words that can hurt, discourage, and end relationships. Technology has enabled people to hide behind text messages and apps and made it easier to insult others within seconds, thousands of miles away, without the thoughts and feelings that come with personal conversation. This, compounded by an overly sensitive politically correct environment, has exacerbated the negative power of words.

At the other end of the spectrum are words that uplift, encourage and empower. We do not hear as much good news as bad because people are too busy paying attention to the media, which thrives on controversies and sensationalism. Everyone understands the power of positive words of encouragement and edification, and would love to receive them, but are too busy to give them.

Bill Britt's message of the power of words is powerfully refreshing in today's world. It is like a vaccine for the young and an antidote for the jaded. You may not be able to control the words coming at you, but you can limit them if they are not positive. More importantly, you can control 100% of the words that come out of your mouth. People join the Amway business to make some extra income and to make their dreams come true. The serendipity is that they get to surround themselves with the most positive, uplifting people they have ever come across. From leaders like Bill Britt, they learn how their own words can shape their future.

Amway is a business opportunity open to people from all walks of life. It is not easy to build a huge Amway business, but it is a simple process. It rekindles dreams. An everyday person starts to dream once again. A dreamer has to deal with naysayers and people that discourage. It therefore follows that along with world class products and a great business opportunity, people need to hear words that teach, encourage, uplift and empower.

Chapter Captures

- Like written words, spoken words are extremely powerful

- We create our future with the words we use. People live at the level at which they speak.

- The power of words has its foundation in the Bible, and is also vehemently promoted by modern self-help books like *The Secret* or *The Law of Attraction*. Most major religions have strong references to the power of the spoken word.

Bill & Kumar onstage during a business conference, using "Verne" to illustrate the power of positive thoughts and words.

Bill was a very strong person, and therefore a very strong leader and ran a very successful business. He was one of the top IBOs because he tended to business and was always on the job. His faith was demonstrated by the way he worked and how openly he spoke to people.

—Rich DeVos

The BWW System

The Story of Amy

The BWW leadership team gave birth, more than four decades ago, to the Britt Worldwide System. Amway offers a business model that enables people to start their own business without the hassles of having to raise capital or quit their primary professions. The idea is to build a team of Independent Business Owners (IBOs), which moves Amway's products into the marketplace. Each IBO's compensation depends on the structure and productivity of their organization. This opens up the opportunities and challenges associated with any team building process, except that in this case, there are no artificial, external limits placed on the IBO. Here is a quick summary of how someone could get started in Amway and move on to become a successful IBO.

Amy is a paralegal in a law office. She makes about $40,000 a year. She has a small baby at home and manages to eke out a living between her baby-sitting costs, commuting costs, other expenses and a demanding job.

Her old friend John from high school finds her on Facebook. After some catching up, John finds out that Amy is looking for ways to get more balance in her life. She could use more money. John offers her the Amway opportunity.

Amy starts her Amway business and taps into the support system offered by her "upline," John and his coaches. She starts to use the products herself and uses the experience of her support team to create customers who buy the products through her personalized retail website provided to her by Amway. She then starts to develop a team. She figures that she is looking for people just like herself, who are ambitious and willing to learn. Three of her friends are not interested, and the fourth one, Julia, only wants to purchase the products, not start a business. However, Julia's brother-in-law, Steven, is a Pulmonologist with a thriving practice. He is also a visiting professor at two very prestigious medical schools. He is not hurting for money, but he is hurting for time. He is looking for ways and means to control it. He has tried but failed with several investments. Julia introduces Steven to Amy, and Steven sees the possibilities in the business and gets started. A couple of weeks later, Steven's wife talks to their UPS delivery guy who is looking to get more out of life. He gets started in the business, too. His wife is Chinese, and so they are able to start a team in China as well. Meanwhile, Amy's niece, who is a college student, gets excited about the opportunity and, in particular, takes a fancy to the XS™ Energy drinks and Artistry™ skin care products. She quickly puts together a team of energetic students for whom even an extra $50 every couple of weeks would mean a lot. Amy's mother signs up as well, but more as a favor to Amy. She does nothing much, but she leads Amy to another lady who is a retired office secretary. She in turn gets in touch with her neighbors, a couple from India, both working in the IT industry in New Jersey.

By now, Amy has a doctor, a truck driver with Chinese connections, a few fired-up students, and a couple of IT consultants of Indian origin on her team. How can she make sure that they all have the opportunity to learn about the products and about business ownership, and pull together to build a profitable business? Amy knows that her security lies in helping others make more money than they are willing to give up. How can Amy relate to such a wide spectrum of people, especially considering that she has no business experience? And what happens when an IBO in China expands into Malaysia, or when the UPS driver in New Jersey talks to a housewife in Los Angeles, who ends up getting started as well? Also, Amy now has three "branches" or "legs," which means she has started three different groups – namely the doctor (who brought in the UPS driver), the niece who signed up her friends, and her mother (who led her to the IT consultants). What happens when Amy starts six more groups? How will she lead, manage and guide all of them?

For answers, let us go back to the 70s. We will look in on Bill and Peggy Britt and see how they got started.

The Seed of a Greater Benefit

We have all heard that failure is the stepping-stone to success. This was certainly true for Bill and Peggy, whose success story is based on what seemed, at the time, like an insurmountable failure.

After his success, Bill used all kinds of analogies and metaphors to make people understand that failure and adversity are an inherent part of success. The only way to become a good piano player, he would say, was to first make a lot of mistakes. Failures were opportunities to grow and learn from, not permanent setbacks or problems.

"You want to see people without problems? I can take you to a cemetery and show you a whole bunch of them! If you are six feet under, you have no problems."

—Bill Britt

Getting into Amway was a great decision for Bill and Peggy. But the opportunity came into their lives thanks to a bad decision Bill had made a few years earlier. Here is the story.

When Bill worked as a City Manager, he had a sign on his desk that read:

"In every adversity there lies the seed of an equal or greater benefit."

That was all fine and dandy, until Bill lost $10,000 in an investment that turned out to be fraudulent. In response to an advertisement he saw in a newspaper, Bill had borrowed $10,000 from a bank for what was supposed to have been an exclusive franchise for eastern North Carolina, selling cars of every make and model. Bill was to get the cars at $50 over manufacturer's cost. But he got nothing. The fact that Peggy supported Bill unconditionally at this time was not enough to keep Bill from losing sleep. For many days thereafter, he would sit in his office, gazing at the sign, wondering what seed of benefit was hidden in this adversity.

Three years later, he received a note from someone named Dale. Bill immediately recognized the name as belonging to someone who had bought into the same fraudulent franchise. In fact, Bill had flown up to New York to meet Dale soon after the fraud had been uncovered to see if together, they could take legal action to recover their losses. When they discovered that "the lawyers were going to take them for more than the crooks had taken them for," they dropped the idea.

In the note, Dale had written the name and phone number of a certain Dexter Yager in Charlotte, North Carolina, who had a business opportunity that could be a means for them to recover their lost investments. Bill promptly discarded the note, deciding that he was not going to take advice from someone "stupid enough" to fall for the same deal he had. However, when Dale called him up to follow up, Bill found himself rummaging through the trash to recover Dexter's contact information.

Bill told this story many times, and it is a great example of his attention to detail, impeccable memory and ability to take quick, comic segues.

"I was told to call you about a business opportunity," he had said in his first conversation with Dexter.

"Yes," replied Dexter. "When can you come down to Charlotte?"

"Look, Mr. Yager," said Bill, "I am a busy man. I am the City Manager here, I command a National Guard unit, and also go to graduate school. So I am calling to find out about this over the phone. I cannot come to Charlotte."

"I cannot explain this over the phone," responded Dexter.

"I live in a glass house. I cannot do anything illegal or questionable."

"There is nothing illegal going on."

"Well, the guy from Buffalo couldn't tell me anything over the phone, and you are not telling me anything either. I guess this isn't for me, so let us forget about it."

"I guess we will have to forget about it, then," agreed Dexter.

Every time Bill shared this story, he would say, "The only problem was that Dexter knew what I was forgetting, and I didn't." That is a signature Bill Britt punch line. No matter how often repeated, it never loses its "punch."

"Can you tell me anything else?"

"Well, I am in the top 2% income bracket in the country. I am 30 years old and retired," said Dexter.

"He is 30 years old and retired. I am 38 and still going to college," thought Bill. Bill immediately adjusted his schedule and decided to drive to Charlotte the very next day.

Bill was a master storyteller. Unless you paid close attention, you might miss the strong messages he packed in short spurts of humor. The next day, as he walked towards his Pontiac Bonneville, he remembered thinking how pretty it had looked under the light when he bought it at nighttime. In daylight, he couldn't believe what he had bought. Bill quickly added this seemingly insignificant detail into every narration of his story, and only those who paid attention understood that it wasn't insignificant at all; rather, it laid a foundation for what was to come later.

As he drove to Charlotte, Bill started to have second thoughts. He felt that he was probably going to lose money again to some stupid scheme. About halfway to Charlotte, he stopped to fill gas. It cost him 29.9 cents per gallon, and he ended up spending five dollars to fill the tank. By then, he had talked himself out of going to Charlotte. So he made a turn back and headed home.

"Right then, I saw a 'NO U TURN' sign on I-85. I don't like the government telling me what I can't do. That sign was all I needed. So I made the U turn. I remember how I scooped up dirt on the front bumper as I headed to Charlotte."

As he parked outside the Yager residence, he decided to hide the cash he had on him. Unable to reach his shoes ("because of my stomach and the steering wheel getting in the way"), he stuck all of sixty dollars under the floor mat. As he walked up the circular driveway he saw two new Cadillacs parked, one of which was a red convertible. He was greeted by "a little fat guy" named Dexter Yager. Bill asked him if he owned the cars in the driveway, and the house. Dexter told him he did. Bill also found out that Dex had quit his job as a beer truck driver. The carpet and furniture in Dexter's house were far better than anything Bill had ever owned. So on that April day in 1970, a 30-year-old high school dropout and retired beer truck driver showed the Amway business opportunity to a 38-year-old qualified engineer, the City Manager of Carrboro, North Carolina, and a full-time graduate student headed for a PhD and a career in academics.

"I was 38 and no one had ever talked to me about a dream. Dex was the first person. I am going to tell you, if you ever get hold of a dreamer for two hours, it will change your life. No question about it."
—Bill Britt

Bill was so excited by the opportunity that he demanded Dexter sign him up immediately. Dexter told him that he wanted to first give him the opportunity to understand how the business worked. He offered to drive to Bill's home and teach him the ropes and help him build a network of customers and distributors. However, Bill assumed that Dex would charge him extra money to do so (which was not true), and insisted on getting started right away. Dex relented, and Bill went to his car to get the $20 to buy a starter kit. "You dummy," he thought, as he rummaged under the floor mat, "here you are again, fighting to give your money away even when he doesn't want it."

On his way home, Bill read the entire Amway Business Reference Guide by propping it up on the steering wheel. He was so excited that he couldn't wait until he got home.

The Amway business does not pay money to recruit people. Income is made by moving products into the marketplace. Without good products that people need and can afford, the business model would not be sustainable. Bill realized that, so he wanted to check out the products for himself.

He took the next day off, and started to experiment with the products "like a mad scientist." He tried out the SA8™ laundry detergent concentrate, except he didn't follow the instructions and ended up putting a whole scoop for a load of laundry (like he was used to, with other detergents) rather than a quarter scoop. He had to clean up a good amount of overflowing suds and soap. He was fascinated by the concentration and quality of Dish Drops™ Dishwashing Liquid. One drop using a toothpick would fill up an entire sink with suds. He shined 12 pairs of shoes with Amway™ Shoe Spray. By the end of the day, he was sold on the business. He knew that the products would sell.

> *"How many seeds in an apple? Eight, 10, 12...? How many apples in a seed? Infinite!"*
>
> —*Bill Britt*

Growing Pains

As mentioned earlier, the Amway opportunity allows one to develop a team of Independent Business Owners, each of whom sells the product to the general marketplace.

The size of the team one desires to build has to do with the size of one's dream. The sales and marketing plan is available for all to study. Based on that, some people choose to build a small business, while others seek to fulfill bigger dreams. Amway itself has some rules that the business owners need to follow, over and above the law of the land. Apart from that, Amway does not interfere with the actual team-building process. Training and motivating people on one's team is up to each leader. Today, the Britt Worldwide system, fully accredited by the Amway Corporation, is an established system of education with proven steps and methods that can help IBOs succeed in business. This system consists of CDs, books, conferences and technology (such as streaming audio and video) that are made available on an optional basis to Independent Business Owners who want to make use of them.

The Britts' Amway business did not have a super-successful start. The first 19 people that Bill spoke to about the business were not interested in either starting their own venture or buying the products as customers. Bill showed the plan to anyone who was willing to stand still. The first person he talked to was on welfare, and Bill thought that he would jump at the opportunity to make some money. Instead, he told Bill that they would take his welfare check away if he made money elsewhere. Among others, Bill showed the plan to the town drunk, another person named "Cat Baby" because he used that name to address everyone, "Smokey the Bear" because he always had a cigar dangling from his lips, and Peggy's hairdresser. People put Bill down, called him names like "soapy" and "sudsy." They laughed at him and criticized him. They accused him of trying to take advantage of others. Bill realized that this was just part of the process. Every insult, every piece of criticism, made him more determined to succeed.

> *"You know how they say don't kick someone when they are down? If he is a winner, go ahead, kick him. And then run for cover. Because I will guarantee you, when a winner is down, he ain't going to be down for long. And when he gets up, something is going to happen. You can count on it!"*
>
> —*Bill Britt*

Quite often, people get started in the business and don't end up really building it. In a team of ten, two or three people will generally be the most productive. Sometimes the process involves going through a few people before you find the ones who really want to sell the products and build a team for themselves. In Bill and Peggy's case, only one couple from their immediate circle of friends, Rex and Betty Jo Renfrow, ended up building a sustainable business. Even today Peggy remembers "the good old days" before and since they started their Amway business, and their special friendship with the Renfrows. Betty Jo has passed since, and Rex lives in Virginia now.

The town drunk, Cat Baby, Smokey the Bear and others led Bill and Peggy to others who eventually led them to their current leadership team. But it was a process that was riddled with failures, frustrations and hurdles to overcome before it led to a success story.

During their first period of growth, Bill Britt and other major leaders realized that, in addition to product knowledge, people needed to develop soft skills and to learn how to present themselves as professional business owners who knew what they were talking about. They were taught how to "dress for success," how to approach people, and people skills, among other things. They needed to be coached and mentored so they could understand business ownership. It was critical that they develop their self-image so they could handle rejections, criticisms and disappointments. All of these required training. People had to be taught to follow the rules, keep sound records, and file taxes properly and in a timely fashion.

The other extremely important aspect of training was the need for IBOs to learn from each other. For instance, a successful IBO living in Greensboro, North Carolina, would be invited to speak to a group in Los Angeles, California. Down the road, someone would be invited to speak in Greensboro. Exposing new IBOs to different speakers with diverse perspectives allows them to derive inspiration from other people's trials, tribulations and triumphs. This system enables people to find others they can relate to and learn from. For example, in Amy's case, Steven, the Pulmonologist, would greatly benefit by attending a training seminar done by another Pulmonologist, Dr. Hal Newball of Johns Hopkins, who built a successful Amway business.

A natural evolution of these seminars was making audio recordings available so that people in different parts of the country and the world could tap into the system. Bill would often recall the early days, when people who came to attend seminars would bring huge reel-to-reel tapes to make recordings for their personal use. These unwieldy machines would be placed either on or near the stage, sometimes numbering in the hundreds. They would click on and off as they ran out of tape, and the owner would run back and forth to change tapes, causing disruption. The advent of cassette tapes was a blessing for the organization. It made perfect sense to set up an organized system in which the talks would be recorded professionally and made available to the IBOs for a small fee. Amway would provide speaker guidelines and specify legal boundaries, and the system would make sure that people received the education they needed at the best possible price.

Since then, cassette tapes have evolved into CDs, and now into audio/video streaming and other cutting edge products. BWW is one of Amway's top accredited systems, making use of state-of-the-art tools and books. Today, people like Amy have the BWW system literally in the palm of their hand. They have a vibrant schedule of events to support them in their local area and their other groups in faraway places. Use of these tools is voluntary, and available to anyone who wants them. Many years ago, an erstwhile CEO of Britt Worldwide was gathering suggestions for a tagline for the BWW system. The first line that came to my mind was "Empowering People Around the World." It is an honor that this has been officially adopted.

Bill Britt is certainly one of Amway's key leaders who successfully created systems of business building with proven track records. His style was not just to develop a sales team. He set out to develop leaders, and did what he could to teach them everything he knew. By all standards, he was hugely successful in his mission. The BWW system has helped create an army of business leaders who not only have uncommon, yet successful lifestyles themselves, but also were able to spawn other leaders.

Wall Street pundits and corporate CEOs have no idea how fascinating the Amway business is and what it does for people. They are even more clueless when it comes to business systems such as BWW. It may be that they think they know it all. Or it may be that no one has told them the story of leaders like Bill Britt.

Well, it is time for that now. Anyone dealing with organizations of any size ought to learn about someone who successfully led a voluntary army of millions around the world, with not just a message of hope, but a plan and a process.

The BWW system was primarily designed for people in the Amway business. The serendipity has been that its principles and building blocks can be adapted to be used in any area of life. The habits taught within the BWW system can add value to each and every person on this earth, whether or not they are involved in multi-level marketing. Today, BWW receives inquiries from many other corporations and industries. Businesses would like to know how BWW leaders have earned the loyalty of so many hundreds of thousands of people around the world. They would like to implement the same kind of unity in their organizations.

As mentioned earlier, the resources provided by BWW and other support systems are available on an optional basis to the IBOs. It is easy to see how a system like BWW helps unify the team globally. Since the teachings are uniform, it is now viable to develop teams across long distances. This promotes the longevity of the business.

A term that we often use in our business is "The X factor:" what happens to your business if you are not able to perform for a period of time?

A great example is the story of John and Jeannie Belle Crowe, who are now Crown IBOs. After building the business to the Diamond level and beyond, John intercepted a burglary in his own house and was shot in the head. He survived, but was paralyzed on one side. The rehabilitation process has been long and arduous. For John, life is a daily struggle. However, during the most critical period, his business sustained because of overwhelming support from the BWW system and its leadership team.

During the 70s, the news of Bill and Peggy Britt's phenomenal success began to spread. Other organizations within Amway became interested in their system. One of them was led by Ron and Georgie Lee Puryear, based in the state of Washington. After obtaining all necessary approvals, the Puryear team became affiliated with the BWW system. This arrangement continued until a decade or so before Bill's passing, during which time they shared great challenges, celebrations and memorable moments. Ron Puryear passed away after a brief health struggle in June 2016.

Yes, there lay a seed of a great benefit in the $10,000 adversity that Bill Britt had to go through, much bigger than anyone could have imagined. But the seed does not readily fall out of the adversity and present itself. It may take some digging, fighting and overcoming. And even when we find it, it is still only a seed. It needs to be tended and nurtured before it can grow. Meeting Dexter Yager and starting the Amway business was just the seed. Before the sweet rewards of success came the struggle of learning, failing, understanding, fighting and overcoming. All this requires diehard tenacity. Or as Bill would put it, "plain, old fashioned guts."

> *"A winner does not know how to quit. A quitter does not know how to win."*
>
> —*Bill Britt*

BWW has been filling coliseums and convention centers in many different countries. People travel far and wide to hear the message of hope. Even though our methods and processes have evolved with time, the childlike excitement and energy of the Britt culture at these events has been unmistakably consistent over the years. In the early days, ladies would dress up in red, white and blue, and men would dress up in pink, white and blue tuxedos (they couldn't find red ones). Referring to the co-founders of Amway, people would sing "Rich and Jay once had a dream" to the tune of "Old McDonald." Pink suits and eagle belt buckles were not uncommon. Often, coliseums full of people would be swaying and singing "God Bless America." They would even light candles to demonstrate how the dream of free enterprise could spread (something a Fire Marshall would not appreciate today).

Server, Not Kingpin

You can guess that the media periodically had a field day with these events. For instance, NBC Dateline did a show with a hidden camera at one of our conferences and attempted to make a mockery of the excitement and high energy that is typical of Amway functions. They referred to us as being "cult-like" and claimed that Bill Britt was an Amway "king-pin" and "cult leader." The implied message that the media wanted to convey was that people were gullible enough to follow someone and his leadership team for decades on end, with no real substance. What they always miss, and never bother to research and find out about, is the amount of love and effort that exists behind the scenes on the part of the leadership team to connect with people, help them understand the business, and get their profits going, long before they show up in huge numbers at our functions. As a matter of fact, we have received inquiries in India from politicians asking us to help them get people to their meetings (they couldn't pay people to come to their meetings, and at the time of this writing, BWW pulls over a hundred thousand people annually in India alone who buy tickets voluntarily and travel extensively to come to our meetings). Make no mistake about it—Bill Britt and his leadership team earned their stripes by serving people and giving to them. Anyone who suggests otherwise is simply ill informed.

Chapter Captures

- If adversity is a fruit, then an equal or greater benefit is the seed. But the seed won't fall on its own and present itself. It will need some digging, cutting or pulling.

- Necessity sometimes creates chaos. Out of chaos comes the need to get organized.

- For a business to be viable, it has to have a product or a service that people need and can afford. However, intangible attributes like a healthy self-image, a good attitude and people skills are critically important. And companies and individuals should invest in developing those attributes. The BWW system provides the tools and the mentorship needed to develop and maintain a mindset for success.

- In our quest for success, we come across naysayers. They could be well-meaning relatives, cynical spectators, or people from the media seeking sensation. We should not spend our energy trying to convince them they are wrong. They are simply not interested in the truth.

*True happiness is
found in the process
of accomplishment,
rather than in the
accomplishment itself.*
                    —Bill Britt

Spirituality: Bill's Faith

Bill's knew people from every possible religious background: Hindus, Christians, Buddhists, Muslims, you name it. While he was very clear about his Christian beliefs, Bill shared his own experiences from his heart, and through that he sought to find unity among the various beliefs. Did people feel offended? Some did. For the most part, any discomfort would quickly dissolve because everyone felt his intent and love.

Bill was a unifier. One of his favorite Bible verses was Proverbs 6:2 ("You are snared by the words of your mouth"). When he talked about this verse, he would often ask people of other religions if they had a similar reference to the power of the spoken word. The unanimous agreement is a great example of how Bill and Peggy lived their lives. They were non-judgmental, and respectful of all faiths and backgrounds.

"I am what I am," Bill would say, "and you can be what you want to be. If I were born into another religion, I'd probably be very strong about it, just like I am now as a Christian." Then he would demonstrate how he could wave his hands about freely, so long as he was not hitting someone else. "Be what you want to be, but don't disparage anyone else's beliefs. If at all, win them over with love, not by force," Bill would say.

His welcoming spirit should not be seen as weakness. Don't make that mistake.

Going Back to the Source

Early in Bill's career, a person challenged him. Accusing Bill of "helping people get rich," he said, "Don't you know that it is harder for a rich man to go to heaven than for a camel to go through the eye of a needle?" Bill asked him if he remembered the door he had entered through. Then he asked the man to leave by the same door. Whether the camel went through the eye of the needle or not, this man certainly left through the doorway! Had he been respectful in his query, Bill would have been gentler.

The truth of the matter was that Bill wasn't quite sure what the answer to the question was. This incident inspired him to really study the Bible. The next time someone challenged him, he wanted to be prepared. Since the core of his business started in and around the Bible belt region, this decision made sense. So he went home, and checked it out. Matthew 19:24 says, "It is easier for a camel to go through the eye of a needle than for a rich man to enter heaven." But then, Matthew 19:26 says, "But with God all things are possible."

Imagine this. You are sitting around a table with Bill Britt and a few other people of different faiths. You are captivated by his delivery and his heart. You want a happy ending, no matter what your religion is. And that is why, when Bill delivers his punchline, "But with God, all things are possible," you join the others in heaving a big sigh of relief. It is the most unified, all religion sigh you have ever heard.

Many religious leaders exalt poverty. Bill assured people that the Bible clearly indicated that poverty is a curse (Deuteronomy 28). One more sigh. At this point, you are hoping that your religious book says the same thing!

An Inclusive Vision

Bill did not feel insecure about being in the presence of people from other religions. In fact, he would tell his Hindu friends that he felt most Hindus live more like Christians than most Christians do, referring to their long-lasting marriages, unified families and strong value systems.

Building a large direct selling business is not a glamorous thing in the eyes of the media and the outside world. That is the only reason why Bill and Peggy have not appeared on the cover of Fortune magazine. That is also the reason why Bill has not been named "Man of the Year" by Time magazine over and over again. To people who understand business, filling coliseums across the globe and teaching millions how to lead a better life is one of the most magnificent things a person can do.

Standing ovations and loud cheering have been constant, normal parts of Bill and Peggy's lives. Bill would always point his forefinger skyward, reminding himself and everyone else that the glory belonged to God.

Bill Britt was a visionary. He had the uncommon ability to cast his vision and inspire others to catch on to it. Good leaders have great visions. Great leaders pass on great visions to others, and inspire them to dream and to lead. Bill used his material wealth to build the dream for others. The Britts' palatial homes, cars, yachts and planes did bring them a lot of luxury, comfort and convenience, but people who know the Britts are aware that they had these things primarily to encourage others to chase their big dreams and think abundantly. Bill Britt was a dreamer, and a great one at that.

"Where there is no vision, the people perish."
—Proverbs 29:18

No Guesswork

In his religious walk, Bill introduced a multitude of people to Christianity. He did it with a lot of love in his heart. He did not hide what he believed in. You never had to guess where Bill Britt stood on issues. He and Peggy gave away millions of dollars to ministries and churches they supported over the years. Bill's love for God showed in his words and actions.

And yet, Bill developed strong relationships with people of all faiths. It was evident that Bill was a strong Christian, but he never treated them any differently because of their religious faith. For instance, as a Christian, he had some obvious concerns about his Hindu friends, ones that he often spoke about. In the end, he would always conclude with something like "Look guys, if you ever hear that Peggy and I, Paul or Angelo have suddenly disappeared [referring to the rapture], make sure you hit your knees and accept Jesus Christ immediately." He did his part by sharing his convictions and beliefs with a lot of love, in a manner that did not offend or alienate those who were paying close attention.

Today, we live in a world where political correctness often overwhelms freedom of speech. Bill Britt spoke his mind and had a huge following of people from every walk of life. He was super-successful in many ways and had the transparent wherewithal to let the world know that he based his life on and attributed his success to Christian principles. Many people appreciated that he was honest about his beliefs and experiences, and did not sugarcoat his delivery with "acceptable" language and carefully scripted words.

Every person of influence has a following based on a common denominator among his or her followers. It could be based on an interest (like country music), a religious belief, a political affiliation, or a myriad of other subjects.

Bill Britt had a following from every walk of life. He had a direct and simultaneous influence on a Seventh Day Adventist Harvard medical graduate, a Sikh farmer in India, a Hindu PhD in Medicinal Chemistry in New Jersey, a Muslim engineer in Michigan, and a Buddhist cook in China. His ascent is showered with love, truth, unconditional giving and transparency. The common denominator among Bill Britt's followers is the dream.

In All Things

Paul Miller remembers an instance where Bill excitedly quoted 1 Thessalonians 5:18 from the Bible: "In all things, give thanks." He repeatedly emphasized the word "all," and explained that this meant we are to be grateful about all things, good and bad. Everything happens for a reason, and we accept every occurrence in our lives with humility and gratitude. Bill lived by this principle. This is one reason why those who knew him have seen his equanimity during the toughest of times. He lived it, and he taught it.

Executive Diamond Charlie Durso's most powerful memory of Bill was in Mexico City, when Ann Durso's pocketbook was stolen along with her four-karat diamond earrings and nine-karat diamond necklace. Bill reminded the Dursos to give thanks, and also taught him about the rule of seven—anything stolen from those with faith will be replaced sevenfold (Proverbs 6:31). And, shortly afterwards, Charlie and Ann were blessed with a windfall of profits approximately seven times the value of what had been stolen.

The Softer Side

Bill took on many issues and problems, and got them solved before they could percolate into the organization. He took pride in shielding the organization from negative situations. These ranged from personal health situations to helping others find solutions to unjust lawsuits. Every once in a while, he would let his guard down and people close to him could see his human side.

Executive Diamonds Wayne and Suzanne Callender once had the opportunity to ask Bill how he was able to handle the hurts that he had experienced over the years. For a few moments, they were able to sense his feelings in the faraway look in his eyes. He acknowledged to them that he just had to find ways to deal with whatever life threw at him. And yes, he did feel the hurts. The Callenders realized that their hero was human, like everyone else.

The lovable thing about Bill's controversial side was that "Teddy Bear" and "Mother Teresa" were just as readily available as the "General Patton" side of his personality. Angelo Nardone recalls a time when Bill apparently said something that deeply affected someone who was listening. Angelo found out about this and talked to Bill, who then invited the person to meet with Bill. After listening to them intently, he said, "Would you forgive me? I had no clue that I had offended you that way, and promise not to do that again." That was Bill Britt.

Sometimes he would go on the offensive about something, and later, when he was alone, wonder about what had happened and whether there was something he could do or change. Once, someone brashly pointed out to him in a meeting that the Bible said that money was the root of all evil. Bill's first reaction was to ask the man if he preferred to leave the room with or without a knot on his head. Later, Bill went home and did some research, and started to educate the so-called "pious" people on what he discovered.

"For the love of money is a root of all evil..."
—*Timothy 6:10*

It was not money, it was the love of money that the Bible preached against.

The softer side of Bill Britt was always around the corner, willing to learn, change and apologize if needed. His ability to forgive was limitless, and he practiced what he preached.

The Motivation Multiplier

The most succinct explanation of the word "Motivation" I ever saw was when Bill defined motivation as follows:

NEEDS x FAITH = MOTIVATION

This formula is not only catchy and easy to remember, but also underlines two very important aspects of a strong spiritual foundation: dreams and faith. Needs arise out of dreams. When a dream is not deep rooted, it is nothing more than a fantasy, since there is no corresponding effort or passion. When a dream becomes a need, it achieves significance. There is a difference between saying "I would like to get out of debt" versus saying "I need to get out of debt."

Faith is belief in the unseen. It is believing in something that is not yet within one's grasp. It is knowing that something not physically present is going to manifest itself, if we act based on our faith.

A big dream with little faith, or a small dream with a lot of faith, will result in little motivation. To accomplish ordinary things, ordinary needs and a little bit of faith would suffice. For example, as a student I had a need for extra income, to be able to make ends meet. I got a gig singing at an Indian restaurant for $3 an hour. I had faith that I would reach the restaurant safely every day, and that they would pay me before I returned home safe. If I did not have the faith, I wouldn't be motivated to act. If I felt that I would not be able to make it to the restaurant safely (this was West Philadelphia), I would not have left home.

Big Dreams need Big Faith. Bill encouraged everyone to dream big and identify needs. He explained that the Faith component was a multiplier of different types of faith:

FAITH = FAITH IN GOD x FAITH IN COUNTRY x FAITH IN AMWAY x FAITH IN BWW x FAITH IN MENTORS x FAITH IN SELF.

He pointed out that if any of these faiths was zero, then the motivation would be non-existent. He explained that faith in God was of utmost importance. The fact that God had created everyone equal makes it possible for someone to say with conviction that "If that person can achieve, so can I." Bill was totally convinced that God had handed people a blueprint for success through His words.

Faith in country was of utmost importance in Bill's world. He explained how it would be difficult to function if we didn't believe in our own country. Regardless of political beliefs, it is important for us to believe in a great future for our country. This gives us hope and makes us want to strive for a better life. Bill was proud of being an American and he reminded people that America was the "hope of the world."

When leaders lead by example with strong foundational principles, people develop faith in their wisdom and advice. This is where the "Faith in Mentors" comes into play.

Finally, Bill concluded that most people did not have a problem with all of the above faiths. The real issue, he said, was the last multiplier – faith in self. He strongly believed that most people did not believe in themselves. Bill dedicated his life to investing in others to help them believe in themselves, and created a process that will live on for a long time to come.

Figure It Out Later

Bill cautioned us against analyzing things too deeply. "Too many people spend too much energy trying to figure everything out before they do something," he would often say. "Sometimes it is better to go ahead and do it and then figure out how you did it." He would make this statement almost flippantly, but it was based on a solid, spiritual foundation of faith. He stressed the importance of seeing things as they can be, not just as they are. This fit very well with his passion for the power of the spoken word. He certainly walked his talk, and repeatedly and consistently acted on faith. Sometimes things didn't work out as he had expected, but most of the time, they did.

A new airport had been built in Sanford, North Carolina while Bill was City Manager. During the inauguration ceremony, the fixed base operator asked him if he had ever thought of flying a plane. Bill decided that if he was going to do something, why not right away? Right after the ceremony, Bill took his first flying lesson. Three days later, after a mere six hours of flying time, he decided he was ready to fly by himself. A couple of days later, Bill bought a 1963 Cessna 172. The plane needed to be moved to Southern Pines, NC, for an engine overhaul. A month later, the plane was ready. Bill still only had six hours of flying time, but nevertheless decided to pick up the plane and fly it back himself. A day later, he decided to fly to Florida with Peggy. The flight to Florida was eventless, but the return had some exciting moments, when Bill had trouble landing the plane because he was only aware of one radio frequency, while the air traffic controller was on a different frequency.

Soon after, Bill, Peggy and an inebriated cousin were on Bill's Super Mooney 21, headed once again to Florida. On the way down, they ran into some heavy clouds. Bill did not have the training to fly in clouds. When the air traffic controller realized that Bill did not have the expertise he needed, he asked him to get out of the clouds immediately, to which Bill responded "You tell me how, and I will do it." There was nothing much the controller could do, so Bill had no choice but to somehow hold steady and make it through. He recalls that the other side of the clouds had the most beautiful view he had ever laid eyes on, because he could actually see what was ahead of him.

On the way back, Bill saw a build-up of clouds moving from west to east. So he decided to move around them by flying east. He underestimated the speed of the clouds and kept flying east over the Atlantic, and decided to turn back when he realized he might run out of fuel. He headed out west, knowing and later hoping that they had to see land soon. "I felt like Columbus, looking for land. My cousin was wishing he had brought some more alcohol with him. Peggy was in the back, happy for a while, and then her eyes grew bigger and bigger." Finally, they saw land and that was, according to Bill, the second most beautiful sight in his life. He admired the fact that despite some anxious moments, Peggy had total faith in him.

> *"I don't recommend that you learn how to fly like I did, but sometimes you don't have a choice. You find yourself in a position where you have to figure things out on the fly. That is when you stay calm, stay focused. Your determination will see you through."*
> —*Bill Britt*

The underlying force behind his equanimity was his faith in God. His off-the-cuff remark that it is sometimes better to do things first and then figure out how they were done was rooted in his belief that when God is in charge, we don't have to worry ourselves.

Zest for Life

In the summer of 2009, Bill and Peggy hosted more than 100 IBOs at their Florida estate. A few months before that event, he decided to discover if he had a singing voice. And he discovered that he did indeed have a singing voice! On that summer afternoon, Bill sang at least five songs on a stage that he had set up on his farm across from his estates. It was hot, and as we discovered later, he was not exactly in the pink of health, but his enthusiasm overcame all obstacles. He sang from his heart, and everyone loved it. Bill gave it a hundred percent, a hundred percent of the time.

When Paul, Angelo, Raj, Kanti and I got together with Bill at his Florida estates for our Management Operating Committee meetings, we would try and finish early so Bill could get to bed, especially during the last few years. Kanti and I would stay in Bill's house. Before he would go to bed, he would make me sing songs, and he would play the piano and sing with me. Initially, I would sing unfamiliar songs like "Mustang Sally" and "I've Got You Under My Skin." Then Bill would play some of the preprogrammed songs on the digital piano and make me pick one. I would pick numbers like "Stairway to Heaven," not exactly his genre, but he would play along with excitement and enthusiasm. We would try and get him to sleep. Peggy would be concerned. But Bill would not let go until he had finished what he set out to do.

At 80, he had the enthusiasm and eagerness of a teenager. He kept up with technology to the extent possible. He learned how to use the latest PCs, the iPad 2 (he would call it the "I 2 Pad" for some reason), and the iPhone. He would often FaceTime with his friends and business leaders. He would keep trying until he got it to work. That was how he lived his life. He never knew how to quit. Nor did he want to know.

"Do not get weary in well doing."

—Galatians 6:9

No matter what the circumstances looked like at any given time, Bill had total faith that he would find a way. He knew that if he could see it in his mind, he could make it happen. He reminded people that the unseen controls the seen.

"A hotel does not get built because an architect met an engineer and a construction worker by accident and they started building it. It was first built in someone's mind. Similarly, you don't rob a 7-11 unless you first think about it. The unseen controls the seen."

—Bill Britt

Bill led a spiritual life. He acknowledged that no one was perfect and everyone is bound to make mistakes. But if we strive to live by godly principles, we will be blessed abundantly.

Steady as a Rock

If one was to compare Bill's talks from the 70s to those from the new millennium or any time in between, it is easy to verify the consistency of his message. The voice changed from that of a young, energetic Bill to a more mature, yet still-energetic, voice over the years. But his teachings were steady as a rock. We have the rare privilege of being able to listen to Bill's recordings from years ago.

Bill's voice changed over the years, the medium has changed from cassettes to CDs to streaming. It is reassuring to see how he stood unwaveringly by the same, steady beliefs and principles.

Diamonds Nick and Parul Soni once asked Bill what the secret to his consistency was. To which he replied, "If you tell the truth, you don't have to remember what you said the last time you spoke."

Time and again, Bill has narrated stories and incidents from the past, facts that corroborate his beliefs, style and consistency. They are mostly off-the-cuff, and not rehearsed. But there were never any inconsistencies. Even when he went off on a tangent, his intentions were never questionable. That steadiness and reliability permeated his life. His friends could count on him. He was always willing to listen and was quick to apologize if he had hurt anyone unknowingly. He knew how to simplify problems and remove the clutter in someone's thinking. When people panicked, he would calm them down. He would lighten the atmosphere before dealing with the issue.

In 1998, Amway opened its India market. People from all parts of the world rushed to India prior to the launch, began talking to others and working to form a network prior to the opening. These activities were against the rules of Amway. Amid this frenzy, a few IBOs in the U.S. who were of Indian origin ran to Bill and urged him to let them break the rules, and do what other people were doing. They feared that they would lose the people of India to other groups. I was there when Bill sat them down.

"Let me tell you the story of an old bull and a young bull. They were grazing atop a hill, when they saw a herd of cows at the base. The young bull was excited, and he said 'Let us run down and get one each!' The older bull smiled and said 'No son, let us walk down and get 'em all!'" He went on to assure them that it would be better to follow the rules and not jump the gun. And he was right.

This is one of the lighter examples of Bill's equanimity. Over the years, he spent countless hours resolving issues, ranging from ego problems between business leaders to more serious situations like couples on the brink of divorce, unexpected deaths or a sick child. One incident stands out. He once found himself in a room full of men carrying guns (he later discovered), livid about the promiscuous behavior of a so-called leader. Bill navigated the tension in the room, and was able to calm everyone down and make sure no one fired at the offender. He remained non-judgmental and was able to propose an acceptable resolution so that people could move on and build their businesses. All the offender needed to do was come clean and apologize. In the end it did not work out, and the person in question ended up leaving the team, but the point is that people counted on Bill Britt to get them through tough times.

His steady calmness had its roots in a strong, spiritual foundation. Bill believed in a kind and loving God, who was always in control. "Let us not worry too much," he once said. "Let us go to bed and get a good night's sleep. God is awake all night anyway. He will show us the way."

> *Fear thou not; for I am with thee: be not dismayed; for I am thy God: I will strengthen thee; I will help thee; I will uphold thee with the right hand of my righteousness.*
>
> *—Isaiah 41:10*

Purpose Driven

Yes indeed, Bill Britt ran a business, and a very profitable one at that. But money was not his driving force. When he gave, he wasn't thinking about what he would receive monetarily. He encouraged people to control money and not let it control them. He taught them how they could do that through owning their own Amway business. He taught them how to make money without compromising on values, principles, integrity and relationships. Whenever there was a doubt as to which way the money had to go, Bill Britt always pushed it away from him and toward the other person. He lived by that principle.

> *"Cars can only get so luxurious. Mattresses can only get so comfortable. Steaks can only get so juicy. After a while, a house is a house and a car is a car. When you leave this earth, you don't take a U-Haul or a tractor trailer with you. You came with nothing. You leave with nothing. Money is simply a measure of service to society. It is neither good nor bad. It is how you make it and what you do with it."*
>
> *—Bill Britt*

Bill would often talk about his purpose in life. He would tell us of instances where he had had some close calls, but was miraculously saved, and he felt God wanted him around for a little while longer. He often joked of an incident when he was driving back home alone late one night. He felt hungry, but all he could find was some peanut butter. He proceeded to stick a huge chunk of peanut butter into his mouth and almost choked to death. Somehow, he managed to dislodge the sticky stuff from his throat.

Another instance he would often recall was how during one of his trips, he had to crash-land his helicopter in the middle of a forest. He would tell us that he was not perturbed or anxious. If his God was ready to take him, he was ready to go. The fact that he remained safe was a sign to him from God that he still had work to do on earth. More recently, he would recall how he died two times on the operating table after he had a split aorta, which is a very serious medical condition. Bill would talk about it like it was a case of the common cold. He was spiritually so strong that he had no fear of death. He was ready to meet his maker when the time came.

> *"His Lord said unto him, Well done, thou good and faithful servant, thou hast been faithful over a few things, I will make you a ruler over many things: enter thou into the joy of thy Lord."*
> —*Matthew 25:21*

Chapter Captures

- Very few people know how to incorporate their religious beliefs into their lives effectively. Many religious leaders try to attract people to their faith by beating them over the head with their religious book. Bill's way was to teach them by example, show them how to link their dreams and goals to a way of thinking that has a spiritual foundation.

- Faith does not have to be a boring obligation. It can be a vibrant, joyous catalyst that promotes physical health, a happy mind-set, great attitude and success in all aspects of life.

- Bill's belief was, when faith is the foundation, fear disappears. You can meet life's challenges without worrying about what will happen, because you are anchored in your faith.

- Being non-judgmental and inclusive is the first step toward winning over others.

Bill with Dexter Yager, the "master dream giver"
who first showed the business plan to Bill in 1970.

Bill & Peggy boarding their jet.

Bill often punctuated his talks with humor. Pictured here in India, Bill demonstrates with these volunteers that they will never forget the experience of having water poured on their heads.

When you talk about leaders who have had a positive impact on the Amway business and the lives of hundreds of thousands of people around the world, Bill Britt is at the top of the list. Bill was a passionate, hardworking, loyal, honest person who cared about people and cared about the values of Amway. Bill is one of the key leaders in expanding the business around the world and his passion for free enterprise touched us all. While we will miss Bill and his passion for the business, his legacy will live on forever because of the strong ethical foundation he has built in his business, as well as the commitment and loyalty he gave to his people around the world.

—Jim Payne, Executive VP, Alticor

The Fighting Spirit & The Extra Mile

Every time he was invited to speak, Bill would do way more than what had been expected of him. He would do his talk and then spend time with those who sought more.

On one occasion, we asked Bill and Peggy if they would join us for a relaxing dinner following an exhausting three-day event. The idea was to let them unwind, and not bother them with questions. A few of us accompanied them. Right in the middle of the main course, Bill stood up abruptly and walked over to a table full of new IBOs. They happened to be eating there as well, and had kept their distance, glancing with awe in our direction, evidently hoping they would be able to shake hands with Bill. Forty minutes later, Bill was still talking to them, encouraging them, and sharing the basic concepts of the business with them like it was the first time he was doing all of it. His passion for the Amway business was unmistakable. Even when exhausted, and despite the fact that he might have shared the same information thousands of times, his face would light up and he would come alive while talking about his passion.

"Bill wanted to be useful and he didn't have any status about it. He could walk on stage and captivate tens of thousands or walk over to a table of six, it didn't matter to him."

—Kevin Bell, Diamond

Even when his health was failing, he would stay up until late at night, just sharing and giving to those who had the stamina to stay up. When he gave to others, he was in the zone, and you couldn't stop him. During his maiden trip to India, Bill was insistent on talking to the Indian leaders late at night, despite a hectic schedule and jet lag. He would fall asleep while talking, but would not quit until he was done. And you guessed it right—the message he had was still powerful.

Even at 80, with a heart and kidney condition, he had the alacrity of a man in his twenties when it came to memory, humor and ability to process information. His enthusiasm was contagious. When he did something, he did it with all his heart. He was not tentative or half-hearted about anything. Once, a few leaders from India were visiting his home. Bill was showing them around, and his home theater would not turn on. Bill continued to talk to them and share his wisdom with them, but he would not quit or leave the room until he could get the theater to work. It took him four hours, but he simply would not quit. At the time, home theaters were rare to find. He knew that making it work would impress his visitors, maybe stretch their dreams a little.

"People are hungry for knowledge. They have questions that need answers. I have spent hours and hours, very often past midnight and until dawn, counseling and talking to people. As long as they are willing to receive, I am willing to give. The only problem is that these meetings make you hungry, and I must have eaten a million eggs and drank two million cups of coffee in this process."

—Bill Britt

Just a few months before Bill passed away, Kanti Gala had arranged for a few hundred people to visit Bill and Peggy at their estate. Bill was not as fit as he used to be, and was moving around in a golf cart. He faced frequent challenges in his breathing. But he had a few things on his mind that he wanted to share with people. This was not a structured meeting, so people came in at different times of the day. Each time a new group arrived, Bill would repeat the message with the same enthusiasm and excitement that he had the first time. He must have done it

15 times on that hot day.

One time, someone asked him if he ever got bored, repeating the same thing over and over again. His response was that leaders had a responsibility to educate people, and that required patience and diligence. In turn, repetition is a very rewarding experience, and the teacher gets better and better each time. He compared this to being a performer in a Broadway show. A good actor would get better each time, fueled by the desire to share his or her talent and improve with each performance. The driving factor in all of this, he would point out, was that while the show remained the same, the audience would be new every single time.

Diamond Al Hamilton recalls an incident when Bill Britt had a night's layover in Detroit on his way back from a long and hectic international trip. He ran into an IBO from Al's team at the airport, and discovered that there was going to be a meeting that night. So instead of going to bed, which would have been totally understandable, he decided to speak at the meeting.

Bill Britt led with passion. He loved his God, his country, his wife and his people. He enjoyed and appreciated all the good he could find in them. He loved to laugh and make others laugh. Even when he repeated a joke, he would deliver it like it was his first time telling it. The same was true of some of his stories and anecdotes. Ardent, diehard Britt kids like me often knew what he was going to say and yet waited for the punch lines, our hearts racing. And we would join him from the audience, saying the words with him as if the lines were meant to be a chorus.

"So then because you are lukewarm, and neither cold nor hot, I will spew thee out of my mouth."
—Revelations 3:16

Powerless, Yet Powerful

A few weeks before Executive Diamond Al Fratantuono's passing in November 2013, he had emailed me the following experience with Bill and Peggy that had a lasting impact on him and Mary Anne.

One time, after a convention in the Poconos, a big snowstorm blanketed the area and took out the electricity in the whole town. The Fratantuonos, the Britts and many other IBOs were snowed in. Bill and Peggy spent the whole time teaching the IBOs about the power of the spoken word. They assured them that Diamonds would come out of that weekend. They were right. Al and Mary Anne became Diamonds within two years. That's the kind of influence Bill and Peggy have had on people.

Rocky Covington, an Executive Diamond on the Britt team, recalls a similar incident. The first time he ever really got close to Bill was in October 1977 at a small leadership function in Gatlinburg, Tennessee. He had only been in the business for a couple of months. He had driven down with a small group of people to this function, not knowing what to expect. Bill and Peggy spoke that Saturday night, but around midnight, the lights in the ballroom went out. The hotel was unable to get them back on, so Bill took a couple of hundred people and went in to the hotel lobby. Bill sat at the top of the stairwell and talked to them until four in the morning. Rocky will never forget people sitting on the stairs, listening to Bill. He remembers telling one of his guys that he had never heard anybody speak like that before.

Not many people will continue to hold meetings when the power goes out. Bill and Peggy got the best out of every moment of their lives. Bill was simply indefatigable. He was a man on a mission and would not back down, no matter what.

Cold, Yet Hot

Diamond Rick Fairchild was just 21 years old when he met Bill Britt for the first time. Bill had flown up to Minot, North Dakota, to do a meeting for Rick and his wife, Toni. Rick recalls how grateful he was for Bill having made such a long trip to talk to a team of just about a hundred people.

As soon as Bill landed, the dry, frigid, winter air caused his nose to bleed. It didn't stop for hours. The bulldog that he was, Bill did a three-hour meeting using a towel that started out white and had turned red with blood by the time he finished. Later, Bill played the piano with a glass of water on his head. At first, Rick could not figure out why Bill was doing this. The message became clear when Bill said, "You will never forget what you saw tonight—a man with a bloody nose, playing the piano with a cup of water on his head. That is in your brain forever!" He meant to remind his audience that the brain was powerful and it records everything you see, good and bad, and that is how thoughts and beliefs are created. He constantly used illustrations like this to make his point, especially with his depiction of Verne.

The Bulldog

Someone once said that Bill Britt was George Washington, Mother Teresa and General Patton, all rolled into one. People who love Bill referred to him fondly as Teddy Bear, the Lamplighter, Big Daddy, the Warrior, and the Big Kahuna. The most popular nickname, however, was "Bulldog."

In the army, Bill's favorite sport was fighting. His broke his nose five different times. Physically, he was very strong. Even in his seventies, he had an iron grip when he shook hands, a grip that would make men twice his size buckle down to the ground helplessly. It was like he was always ready for a fight.

While at school, Bill was unable to take part in sports because he was too busy supporting his family by working multiple jobs. Otherwise, Bill could have been an incredible athlete, probably a linebacker in football. His shoulders and forearms were powerful. One time, about ten men tried to shove Bill into a swimming pool. Result? Ten wet men, one dry.

Executive Diamonds Chak and Uma Kakani remember being in a hotel elevator with Bill one afternoon in Dallas, Texas, accompanying him to his suite. On the way up, a WWF (now called WWE) wrestler got into the elevator. One thing led to another and Bill found himself challenging him to an arm wrestling match and dared him to step out of the elevator. While some might consider this foolhardy, Bill's confidence was not entirely misplaced; his arms were unusually strong, and we have witnessed him bring people twice his size and half his age to their knees with his iron grip. In any case, the burden of separating the WWF wrestler and Bill Britt fell on Chak, who assured Bill that he was only trying to protect the other guy!

When it came to fighting for his dreams or his people, Bill Britt was unstoppable. As a young boy, he had to fight for survival and work every day to fight poverty. He had to fight the trauma of dealing with an alcoholic father. Later, he fought for his country in Korea. He dealt with his own failures in and out of the Amway business until he succeeded. His most significant struggle and success was in the Amway business, a super-successful fight for his personal, economic freedom. Once he made it big, he had other fights, and the ones that really got under his skin included some of the frivolous lawsuits successful people often have to deal with. No matter what the nature of the fight was, Bill never backed down. He just knew that in the end, justice would prevail. When he had been in the military, defending his country, he knew he would win. In the Amway business, the first 19 people he showed the plan to were not interested. But Bill grew even more determined to succeed. And he did. Challenges were something that had to be dealt with, not ignored or run away from.

"To succeed in life, you have to learn how to deal with crap. When you come across it, you find a way around it, under it, above it, or through it, but you come out OK on the other side of it, until you find the next pile of crap to deal with."

—*Bill Britt*

His last few years with us were riddled with his constant battle with his health. He was admitted into hospitals several times during that period, often in serious condition, but he would somehow fight his way back. But for the fact that no one can live forever, Bill would have been back home from his last visit to the hospital as well. He lost his physical fight on January 23, 2013, but based on his faith, it was also the most successful day of his life.

Bill fought for what he believed in. Once, while in an airplane, someone was being loud and offensive, going on and on with four lettered expletives and abusive language. That day, this person got a sample of General Patton and the Bulldog. Mother Teresa was absent. Bill almost drove his fist, backed by 220 pounds, into the offender's face. The captain intervened and escorted the individual off the plane.

One time, Diamonds Kevin and Beth Bell were at a coliseum function and Bill was not feeling well. This was around the time he started to develop symptoms of heart trouble. His energy level was obviously low. But he was not about to give in. As his name was being announced on stage, he started to walk toward the podium and all the Diamonds backstage watched as a transformation came over him. He gained energy with every step and gave one of his most incredible talks. Kevin distinctly remembers that his concern for Bill turned to awe; God spoke through him in a miraculous way that night.

In one of his talks, Bill's central theme was "It's not the size of the dog in the fight, it's the size of the fight in the dog that matters." Diamond Vishal Jain made this talk part of his "regular mental diet." His wife Sonika recalls how Vishal would pop this talk into his car's audio player on the way back from a "no-show" or a business plan presentation that did not result in a "yes." To this day, the Jains carry a copy of this talk in each of their cars.

If you were his true friend, Bill had your back. Loyalty to his people was of utmost importance to Bill. As a friend, if you were in trouble, the first thing Bill would do was fight for you and support you. Even if your trouble was self-inflicted or simply your fault, Bill would first work on getting you out of your situation instead of judging or giving you a speech. You would never have to guess where Bill stood when it came to supporting the people he cared for. He stood on the side of forgiveness, love and loyalty. He was never so dogmatic about his principles that there was no room for imperfections and human error.

As mentioned earlier, the Amway business, when built properly, is one of the most fascinating, challenging and fulfilling exercises in team-building and relationship management in the history of the world. Since the multi-level business model is rarely taught in schools, most people who look at the opportunity for the first time do not understand it right away. The real challenge is to educate people as they come along. Teaching people to think outside the box can be challenging and often feel like a fight. To build any successful business, people need to make presentations and face rejections. The rewards of building a successful Amway business are uncommon. It can give someone a great degree of freedom and economic control over their own lives, unlike any other business. And it takes a lot of effort. Many people view their Amway business as their last hope of financial freedom, and the process of building it as their great fight for freedom. Bill Britt has been one of the most effective leaders in that fight.

> *"When I was in the military in a uniform defending this country, I believed we would win. I am not advocating a fight, but we have to fight many fights if we want to succeed. For instance, the only reason we are free today is because somebody died. Someone put it on the line. Someone developed total commitment and went to the battlefield and lost their blood. Freedom is not free. Success is not free. There is a price to pay. That is why many will not succeed."*
> *—Bill Britt*

Because of his father's alcoholism, Bill spent a few years living with his grandfather while growing up. His advice to Bill was "to do whatever it takes, and then a little more." That became Bill's motto. As a City Manager, he would stay back after work while the others went home. In the Amway business, he was willing to outwork everyone else. Bill didn't just go the extra mile. He lived there. He fought sleep to give away a part of his life to another. He fought mediocre thinking all his life and dedicated himself to helping people get rid of what he called "stinkin' thinkin'." He traveled extensively to identify and reach out to dreamers all over the world, giving up the comfort of his luxurious homes to sit in a red-eye flight or drive all night.

In the 70s, the FTC put Amway under a microscope. Top leaders like Bill Britt and Dexter Yager were obvious targets for the media, critics and alarmists.

These great leaders always took events in their stride and never let them change their focus and determination. Diamond Marshall Johnson recalls some important advice he got from Bill: "Decide what you are going to stand for and stand for it. Unless you have something to lose, you don't have a reason to fight."

> *"If you never got sued, or if no one ever wrote or said anything negative about you, it is because you ain't done nothin' yet!"*
> —*Bill Britt*

The Bulldozer

Bill had a lot of hired help to run and manage businesses, as well as various properties, aircraft, cars and other things. However, at the age of 80, and not in the prime of health, Bill acquired a bulldozer and decided to operate it himself to make a pond on his farm property!

Now, why would he do that?

Believe it or not, it all goes back to a dream. One reason Bill joined the army was that he was promised that he would be allowed to operate a bulldozer. However, as we know from his story, Bill was quickly identified as leadership material and promoted to officer level. As a result, this rather strange dream remained unfulfilled for decades. So he decided to fulfill it. End of story.

The Big Promoter

Bill knew how to promote. If he really believed in product or idea, you would know about it. His passion for his conviction was such that if he were promoting a shampoo, even bald people would get excited. Many of his passions were temporary whims, but they had a permanent effect on some people. At one Britt event, Bill was promoting vegetarianism. He had just turned vegetarian himself, and he was flaunting the benefits. He had a few vegetarian IBOs come up on stage to provide testimonials to corroborate his newfound belief. This happened over 15 years ago. Many IBOs turned vegetarian that weekend, and to this day, they are still vegetarian. However, Bill found other facts that convinced him to switch back to eating hamburgers and chicken a few weeks later. It was not that he was fickle. He was very trusting when he came across new information. And while he believed the information, he believed it with all his might. Just like his laughter, his belief was contagious. In any case, these vacillations only happened with relatively trivial topics like vegetarianism, ozone water, coral calcium and colon cleansing. When it came to keeping his word and his promises where it really mattered, Bill was as close to perfect as you can be.

Being the visionary he was, Bill Britt was able to look into the future in a way that few others could. He would talk about Amway going online and becoming an e-commerce enterprise years before it actually happened.

Good business leaders create a vision, articulate the vision,
passionately own the vision, and relentlessly drive it to completion.
—Jack Welch

Keenly Aware

Bill went the extra mile not only in his actions, but also in his attention to what was happening around him. He had remarkable awareness and intuition.

He was a problem solver. He saw solutions everywhere. An observer would find him to be extremely wise, and delightfully entertaining. The entertainment came from his timing and choice of words. During his maiden visit to India, I was sitting next to him in the special high security SUV (complete with a battalion of armed commandos both in the car and on motorcycles) that BWW India had organized for him. He looked at a construction site and made observations that only a keen, sharp mind can figure out within just a few seconds:

"You know Kumar, there are about 20 construction guys there, and four of them are working. 16 of them are doing nothing but watching. If I were the City Manager here, I would fix the place in six months. I know exactly what to do!" I believed him.

He appreciated anyone with entrepreneurial spirit. At the Taj Mahal in India, a photographer observed how popular Bill was and took a few close-up shots. The next day, thousands of copies of these pictures were being sold outside the BWW meeting venue where Bill was the featured speaker. BWW staff was concerned because both Amway and BWW have policies and restrictions on what can be sold to IBOs. It was a legitimate concern. However, Bill appreciated the aggressive spirit of free enterprise behind the selling of the pictures.

> *Bill Britt represented the epitome of the 'Man of Steel and Velvet'. People followed him because they trusted him completely.*
> —*Jody Victor, Founders Council Member, Amway*

Chapter Captures

- People who don't stand up for something will fall for anything.

- Things will begin to happen in our favor when we are willing to fight for something that we strongly believe in.

- Steps can be taught, but heart can only be caught.

- People who live in the extra mile are not looking for shortcuts.

- The "secret" to success is going the extra mile in the way we act, think, dream, speak, listen and love.

Bill & Peggy attending an Indian wedding celebration in traditional dress, and (below) Bill and a group of BWW leaders visiting the Taj Mahal.

Bill onstage dancing to "I Feel Good."

"Joie De Vivre"

The Gourmand

One of Bill's favorite topics was food. He liked to eat, and it showed. He was also constantly reminding himself and others about the importance of eating well. I remember one instance when Bill invited me and a few others to fly to California on Amway's Learjet 60 for a meeting. We talked during the flight, and the topic invariably came to food. Bill started to talk about the fundamentals of eating and feeding, and about the importance of breast-feeding. This was around the time Amway was transitioning to e-commerce.

Later, at the Britt event in California, there were an unusually large number of technology people from Silicon Valley attending a BWW event for the first time. Everybody waited with bated breath for Bill to start talking. They were eager to hear about the big move to e-commerce. Needless to say, they were a little taken aback when Bill's opening topic was the importance of breast-feeding. It was hilarious! Of course, after the shock and awe, Bill conducted a great meeting talking about the importance of staying abreast (pun unintended) of cutting-edge technology and how the Internet would revolutionize the business.

On the way back to New Jersey, Raj Shah had organized some masala dosas, a South Indian delicacy. Bill enjoyed the food. He had not had much exposure to Indian food until the Asian Indian team, led by Kanti and Lata Gala, started to gain momentum in BWW. Indian food became one of his all-time favorite cuisines after that. Bill also fell in love with the Indian people. He really appreciated their value system and the way they treated their elders.

Food was Bill's weakness. He would talk a lot about eating healthy and then reach out the next minute to a piece of cheesecake or some apple pie. If you ever tried to stop him or remind him of practicing what he preached, he would brush you off with something like "Hey, I am not perfect, okay?"

Angelo Nardone and his team in New York were Bill's connection to the Italian world. Some of his best memories were from his visits to New York. The Italian BWW contingent, which includes names like Ray Melillo, Charlie Durso and Vinny Pappalardo, always showed Bill a great time with large amounts of Italian food and desserts. Angelo and his team knew that a cannoli was the perfect way to stop Bill in his tracks. Often, Bill would be talking to someone for hours on end and the leaders around him knew that he needed a break. You can't just walk over and ask someone like Bill Britt to stop talking. What you need is a cannoli.

"I have never eaten anything I couldn't reach."

—Bill Britt

Stickler for Perfection

Bill took very good care of his possessions. Each one of his dozens of cars was spick and span and meticulously maintained. His offices were always organized and clutter free. He took pride in his attention to detail. He spent considerable time planning and directing the artistic landscape around their homes, particularly their estate in Florida. It was as if he knew every rock and shrub intimately. If something were even slightly amiss, you could be assured that the contractor was going to receive a phone call. When it came to business meetings, he would make sure that his employees used the best resources available, no matter the cost. He invested millions of dollars in keeping his audio-visual equipment up to date.

On stage, Bill would often talk about the importance of grooming and appearance. He taught by example. His shoes were always in "spit shine" condition, as he put it. His suits fit him perfectly, and his hair was always perfectly groomed. He would emphasize that it was not about the price tag, but feeling good about oneself and preparing for success.

Music

Bill and I shared another special connection: music. He appreciated my singing and would make me perform at different events. My favorite musical times with Bill were by his piano in his Florida home. Just a few years before he passed on, Bill developed a passion for singing. He would sing songs like "I've Got You Under My Skin" by Frank Sinatra and "Mustang Sally" by Wilson Pickett. He would ask me to sing along.

Bill would often sit at his computerized piano and pretend he was playing while in reality it would be one of the pre-programmed compositions. Onlookers would walk in awe toward him and stop cautiously a few feet away. Sometimes it would take them several minutes to realize what was going on.

At one BWW function, Angelo had him sing to the crowd. Bill was prepared with the music and the lyrics, and the people loved it.

Mustang Sally

The first time I heard Wilson Pickett's rendition of Mark Rice's 1965 song "Mustang Sally" was when Bill played it for me in his Florida home. It has a catchy tune, and Bill had it playing on his computerized "Karaoke" piano. This allowed him to play the notes and sing along. Before I knew it, he had me singing along with him.

Shortly thereafter, a little, cuddly, smart and sweet-tempered dog joined the Britt family. Bill named her "Mustang Sally." She became daddy's girl and adored Bill to no end. Sally would follow him everywhere he went. On occasions when he had to leave her behind, she would run all the way behind the car or the golf cart and only stop short of the invisible electronic fence. She became Bill's best friend and added immense joy to his last few years.

Recently, during one of our visits with Peggy at the Florida home, we decided to watch one of Bill's classic talks on DVD. As soon as she heard his voice, Sally's ears perked up and she sat upright on the sofa, looking for her daddy.

Now Sally has taken to Peggy. She sleeps in a pen by Peggy's bed, and keeps her company, along with two Himalayan cats, Fluffy and Buffy.

Cutting Edge

Diamonds Kankan and Samina Bhattacharyya fondly recall that Bill was always like a kid around cars. He would ask questions about each and every feature and the gadgets and gizmos in them.

One time, they had the opportunity to host Bill and Peggy and drive them around. Bill was fascinated by an FM transmitter in their car, which could be used to play any iPod or MP3 device via the radio. Bill asked Kankan how much he had paid for it, and immediately asked Peggy to pay the $30 and bought it from Kankan on the spot. Kankan tried to not take the money, but Bill insisted. Another time, Bill liked the "blind spot" indicator lights on the Bhattacharyyas' Honda Odyssey minivan, and immediately ordered the latest model for himself.

Bill was not intimidated by change. He anticipated and welcomed anything that he perceived would make life easier and better. While many were skeptical, he was excited about herbs and supplements, and strongly encouraged Amway to expand its Nutrilite brand to include them. Long before personal computers became popular, Bill invested in one, mainly to be able to access different parts of the Bible quickly without having to flip pages. Amway went online in 1999. Bill had started talking about it two years before that. Many business owners his age have a tendency to resist technology and distance themselves from anything hi-tech. Bill, on the other hand, stayed up to date with his iPhone, iPad, FaceTime and Skype. At 80 years of age, with a nasal cannula for oxygen, Bill would Skype with his leaders, and with their children. One of his last video calls was to Kanti's grandson, who was just five years old at the time.

Bill has always led the charge for change. Under his leadership, BWW has developed some of the best technology products in the industry.

Bill often told a story about a boy who noted that his mother would cut off the edges before cooking her ham. When he asked about it, his mother's response was "I don't know, that is how grandma does it." The boy approached his grandma, and got a similar response from her: "I don't know, but that is how my mother did it." Determined to find an answer, the boy went up to his 90-year-old great grandmother and said, "Gray Grandma (great grandma), why did you cut the ham on both sides before you cooked it?" The wise old lady pointed a crooked finger at the boy and said in a quivering voice "Oh! That was because the pan was too small!" This story pretty much sums up Bill's attitude toward the need for change. He encouraged people to think out of the box and challenge the status quo.

Thom Cox, who has worked with the Britts for several decades, noted that

Bill persistently pursued the idea of forever being both the wide-eyed student and the enthusiastic teacher. He added that Bill was always inquisitive and when he encountered an idea of merit, it was impossible for him to keep it to himself.

Live, Laugh, Love

One of his favorite funny stories was from the time he was a City Manager. The Mayor of the city, who was a little hard of hearing, also owned a gas station and would work there on the weekends. One day, two old ladies drove up for gas and asked him if there was a restroom they could use. The mayor thought they were asking for a whisk broom. "Yes, of course, I am sure I saw one this morning," he said to them. "Let me find it for you." The ladies were confused when they heard this, but they were completely aghast when he came back and told them, "Sorry ladies, I was so sure I had one here in the morning, but I can't seem to find it now. But if you would be so kind to step out of the car, I will be glad to use my air hose and blow it out for you!" I must have heard this joke a hundred times, but would find myself falling to the ground, laughing uncontrollably every single time.

Another favorite he often related to his audience was about the guy who got drunk and couldn't find his car. He called his wife and asked her to pick him up at the intersection of "WALK" and "DON'T WALK."

Bill often related a particularly hilarious incident from his childhood. His cousin had talked him into stealing watermelons from a farm. While they were in the middle of their mission, the owner came out with a shotgun and fired a couple of shots in their direction. Bill remembers running so fast that he couldn't even feel his feet on the ground. "I don't have any witnesses," he would say in his inimitable style, "but I guarantee you that on that day, I ran a four minute mile."

Bill was one of the very best at what he did, and he taught well. One of his idiosyncrasies was that if someone discussed any cutting-edge issue or topic that piqued his interest just before he went on stage, there was a strong chance that Bill would bring it up in his talk. Once, someone shared jokes about a politician before he went up to speak, and Bill felt compelled to share them with the audience. It was awkward, but then again, that was Bill.

While Executive Diamonds Vinny and Dayna Pappalardo were Emeralds, they had an opportunity to pick up Bill and Peggy from the airport. They were nervous and excited and left for the airport well ahead of schedule to make sure they got there on time. They left no stones unturned, and were waiting at the gate an hour in advance, holding a beautiful bouquet of flowers for Peggy. It was perfect, except for one tiny detail: they were at the wrong terminal. By the time the Pappalardos realized their mistake, Bill and Peggy had been waiting for over 30 minutes outside their terminal. Instead of being upset, Bill had a hearty laugh and turned the situation into a funny story that he would continue to tell everyone he met that weekend. In his own way, he taught the Pappalardos that what they deemed a crisis was only a minor situation that should be laughed about. This was a timely lesson, considering that Vinny and Dayna were going through frustrations in their business and their lives at the time.

Sometime in 2011, I got a phone call from Bill. "Hey Kumar," he said, "You owe me forty thousand dollars." I simply waited for the punch line. "I bought the Falcon 50 because of you, and now this is what one little maintenance procedure is costing me!" He was jokingly referring to the fact that I kept insisting he get a jet of his own during his later years, especially since he had owned different aircraft when he was younger. He finally ended up buying the Falcon 50. It was the biggest jet he had owned and needless to say, it came with fees for full-time pilots, hangars and other related expenses.

A week later, he called me. "I am glad I listened to you. That plane is somethin' else. I have you to thank for my painless travel."

Once, at a festival in Jacksonville, Bill purposely bumped into a 6'6", 300-pound man and said to him, "Hey, buddy … you wanna fight?" The big, burly, tattooed man looked at Bill and said, "What did you say?" Bill said, "I said, do you wanna fight?" Luckily, the man could tell Bill was kidding, so he said, "No I don't wanna fight," so Bill said to him, "It's a good thing you don't wanna fight because I was gonna turn my boy loose on you!" "His boy" was Rick Fairchild, who has always been skinny, maybe not even half the size of the burly man!

The Italian Connection

Angelo Nardone is a sharp thinker and is always working hard to make things better for all IBOs. He is selfless and always serves the bigger team. He is also the number one prankster in BWW. If you are using the restroom at a BWW function and the lights go off, it is probably not the power grid. If you run into a pile of furniture when you open the door as you leave the restroom, you might as well throw your hands up in the air and sigh "Angelo…"

Bill was always game for a good prank. Angelo recalls the time he and other Italian leaders took him shopping at a special clothing store in Manhattan. They were all dressed in tuxedos following a BWW function. Before Bill entered, they told the owner of the store that they had to check the place out for security reasons because "the Don" would be coming. Obviously that caused some excitement. While Bill was trying on clothes, they connived with the staff and stuffed clothing from the shop into his winter coat. As he was leaving the store, he set off the alarms, and everyone had a great laugh when security "discovered" socks, ties and underwear in Bill's coat pockets.

Angelo is also a great teacher and storyteller. And boy, can he make you laugh! At the MOC meetings, Ang and I are the main joke tellers, and Bill would always look forward to hearing what we had to offer. "Hey guys, we need a break," he would say after an intense meeting. "You have a joke for me?" Sometimes the break would last several hours. We would be laughing like hyenas. That is part of the Britt culture.

The richness of the BWW heritage is evident from the fact that memories created decades ago still bring big smiles to our faces, even to those of us who were not part of the team then. In 1985 (that was the year I came to the U.S. to attend college, just to put things in perspective), Ray and Joanne Melillo (now Executive Diamonds) got married. Surprisingly, Bill and Peggy were able to attend the wedding despite their hectic schedule. Bill had been repeatedly told to expect great food, lively music, dance…and a fight! Yes, a fight. Someone (I believe it must have been Angelo) had convinced him that at every Italian wedding, a fight would break out. Apparently the fight was one of his main motivations to attend the wedding. To accommodate this desire and expectation, and true to his reputation, Angelo went ahead and arranged for one to take place. He asked Ray and, against his better judgment, Ray thought it would be fun to stage a fight between a couple of their IBOs. Anything for Bill. However, here's where he messed-up…the first of many mistakes that a young husband should never make…he forgot to tell Joanne.

After a few hours of dancing and sweating right through to his tie being soaked, Bill came to their table. He leaned over to Angelo and said, "So, where's the fight? I'm loving the food and dancing but, seriously, everyone is getting along here!" Right at that moment, in the middle of a perfectly fun Tarantella (a famous Italian group dance), two of the IBOs on the team began to bump into each other. Then they began to slap each around and wrestle one another to the floor! Angelo gestured to Bill, "There ya go! It's on!" Bill got excited. He stood at the edge of the dance floor and began rooting for them. "Get 'em! Get 'em! Punch him!" It got crazy. The worst part was that Joanne's family had no clue what was happening. As it stood, they were not crazy about Amway in the first place. All of a sudden, with complete horror on their faces, her big cousins came flying across tables to break up the fight! What was supposed to be a fun and playful skirmish became a brawl! Everyone started screaming, the music stopped, old ladies looked like they were going to faint, it was just like in the movies! "It's just a joke!" yelled Joanne, as she tried to break up the fight. As one can imagine, that didn't go over too great with Joanne's family. Afterwards, they were like, "See, these Amway people aren't so nice! How can they start a fight at a wedding?" Even Peggy was totally appalled until it was all explained to her. But in the end, all that mattered was that Bill loved it. Looking back, this wedding became one of the best memories he enjoyed in his Amway career and he mentioned it many times on stage over the years. He got a ton of laughs and brought joy to many people while telling that story.

Giving, Spending, Investing

When Bill talked about his experiences with money, it became clear that depending on the situation, he could be described as being any of the following—generous, discerning, naïve or frugal. When it came to charitable causes, Bill was extremely generous. He never made a big deal of the money he gave away, but he was appreciative of the fact that Peggy and he were able to donate large sums of money to churches and other Christian causes. He would often talk about the million-dollar donation that they made to Duke University for heart research. The Britts' generosity was obvious in the way they hosted and treated their family and friends.

When it came to lifestyle, Bill always went first-class. He was very good at finding bargains for the very best things. He was always ready and willing to sweep up a good deal, ranging from antique furniture to automobiles to yachts, planes and houses. It was apparent that he was very discerning when it came to concrete purchases.

His discernment seemed to be replaced with naiveté when it came to many of the investments he made. In his own words, he had invested millions of dollars with people who were nothing but scam artists, and many of these "ventures" ended in losses and/or lawsuits. Some of them resulted in positive outcomes, but not without a hefty price. He was trusting, and people took advantage of him.

While some of these investment proposals seemed legitimate at first, others were downright funny. One of them was an oil well, which required an investment to dig, almost immediately followed by another investment to fill the well back up, due to regulatory issues. Needless to say, there wasn't any oil.

"Make 'Em Select" was the name of a thoroughbred that supposedly had the potential of winning every horse race on the continent. Bill Britt and a few of his closest friends made a handsome investment and headed out to Seattle to watch the first race. They were excited and optimistic and had access to the club room. Seated in the finest seats in the arena, they waited with bated breath. This was to be the beginning of a new chapter of their lives, since they knew nothing about horse racing. The beginning also turned out to be the end, because "Make 'Em Select" fumbled, fell and broke his leg right after the starting bell went off. In due course, the leg was operated upon successfully, but then the thoroughbred developed a bleeding problem, and had to be put to rest. While we recognize that this could not have been funny at the time for the investors and certainly not for the horse, it makes for a hilarious anecdote, the perfect script for a slapstick comedy.

Bill would often call himself a "cheapskate." He took pride in the fact that he did not care for brand names and fancy apparel. He would boast that he had only a few good quality suits, and none of them cost him more than a couple of hundred dollars. As mentioned earlier, Bill went first-class when it came to "big" purchases like homes, yachts, jets, cars and furniture. But curiously, this did not apply when it came to renting things, traveling on commercial jets or eating at restaurants. Prior to buying his jet, Bill insisted on traveling economy class on domestic flights. He complained that first class domestic travel was a scam. "They put you a few seats in front of the others, and give you almost the same level of bad service, and charge you an arm and a leg for it," he would say.

Diamond Madhu Chheda recalls the time her husband Pravin (who passed away in 2007) was invited to Florida with a few other business leaders for a meeting with Bill. The buffet at the host hotel cost $35 per head. That was too expensive for Bill. He took the team to a place outside where it cost them only $18.99. Bill told Pravin that he preferred buffets because he could eat all he wanted, and he did not have to tip anyone!

Once, Al and Mary Ann Fratantuono accompanied the Britts to a Costco in Florida. Bill was like a kid in a candy store, running between the little stalls with the free sample food. "Can't beat free lunch," he declared repeatedly. However, while heading to the checkout line, he had a cart piled with multiple packets of all the food he had sampled.

Footnotes

Bill loved to dance, and had a talent for it. There were some songs that he could simply not resist the urge to dance to. One of them was "I Feel Good" by

James Brown. As soon as he heard the first few notes, a big smile would light up his face. Then he would bite his lower lip, and go on to sway, caper, twirl and jig with the nimbleness of a fawn. Signature Bill Britt. At BWW weekend functions, this song became a tradition, especially when Bill entered stage on Sunday afternoon to wrap up the event.

Diamonds Tom and Estelle Joachim remember spending a few days at the Britt Estates in Florida. One night, they sang karaoke until the wee hours of the morning. A special song came on and Bill grabbed the microphone and said, "Come here, Peg, they are playing our song!"

"It was magical," says Estelle. "Bill and Peggy started to dance. It was as if time came to a standstill. They were like newlyweds doing their first dance, lost in each other's arms and eyes, with the occasional giggle or two."

"Have you ever heard of the phrase 'Catching lightning in a bottle?'
Growing up, we thought it was just a myth or a fairytale and then
we met a very special man.....and we knew it was true....lightning
could be harnessed and contained and its name was Bill Britt."
—*Tom Joachim, Diamond IBO*

Chapter Captures

- "Joie De Vivre" means "Joy of living." Life is not about not having challenges. It is about staying joyous and cheerful for the most part.

- While we should be sensitive to others, we cannot be perfect. It is important for us to be able to speak freely, as long as our intentions are pure. We cannot let political correctness paralyze us.

- We should all strive to live life a hundred percent and more. If you want to drive a bulldozer, do it! Life is limitless and your dreams are there for the taking.

- Spread cheer and joy. Don't be afraid to surprise others or be surprised.

Bill with friends and fellow Diamonds during a wedding reception.

Kumar with Mustang Sally,
Bill & Peggy's devoted pup,
at their Florida estate.

The piano played a big part in Bill Britt's life, both as a toddler (above) and as a great source of entertainment at his Florida estate.

Bill & Peggy at the grand piano at The Lodge,
their estate in Chapel Hill, North Carolina.

Bill onstage at a business conference in Europe. The "American Dream" of personal business ownership has spread to millions around the globe.

Britt Hallmarks

Shock and Awe

We called them Brittisms. They were things he would say that would ruffle feathers, wake you up, and make you do a double take. They certainly were attention grabbers. Here are a few examples:

1. About the huge potential of the Amway business:
"If I make more money in a day sleeping until noon than you do working all year, then one of us is stupid…. And it ain't me!"

2. On finding the right mentor:
"If you want to be broke, find a nice broke person and take them out for coffee. Make sure you have your note pad and recording device with you. After you order the coffee (and you pay for it, because he won't), ask this person to tell you what exactly he did to become broke. Write down every word he says, and record the entire conversation. Go home and follow his advice to a tee. I guarantee that you will be broke shortly thereafter."

3. On ignorance:
"Some people cannot find their rear end with both hands in broad daylight."

4. To put formal education in perspective:
"Some people need a PhD to figure out how to live on that paltry income."

Bill was a conservative Christian and did not try to hide it. That was what made him who he was. In this context, I have an interesting observation. Over the past few years, BWW leadership has not touched upon the sensitive issues that Bill used to thrive on. We felt the need to change with time. For instance, we have a lot of people in their twenties getting into our business, and living together seems to be the norm for them. What is amazing is that a couple of 20-year-old IBOs found Bill's old cassettes from a yard sale somewhere. Based on what they heard on those tapes, they decided to get married, and encourage others to do the same. These talks from yesteryears resulted in at least three weddings in the couple's organization. Not long ago, these kids came up to me and asked me why other BWW leaders were not teaching this anymore. How about that?

> *"We loved his bold approach and his stand on life truths but sometimes, he'd go right to the edge of our mental ability to tolerate him. It felt like we hated to love him.... or loved to hate him! But the one thing we could not do was ignore him."*
> —*Ray Melillo, Executive Diamond*

A Flying Leap

To help people speak words of victory, Bill would often have the audience repeat things after him.

"I am a winner. I am making it happen. I have a bell to ring, and I will ring it. I have a song to sing, and I will sing it. I am going Diamond. I will not be denied..." he would chant, pausing between the sentences to allow the audience to repeat the words. The rising crescendo would conclude with a chorus of a punch line that became a hallmark of Bill's teachings:

"...And if somebody doesn't like it, they can take a flying leap!"

"A Flying Leap" is a signature Britt term. It signifies the fact that true dreamers are not affected by naysayers and dream stealers. It is symbolic of a stand that a winner takes when it comes to facing criticism and rejection. It inspires the Britt student to "keep on keeping on."

Sometimes, Bill used "hide in the bushes and watch" instead of "take a flying leap." The basic message is that success is not attained by trying to win a popularity contest. When someone sticks their head out of a crowd, people will throw stones at them. If your dreams are clear and you believe in yourself, none of the naysayers will have an effect on you.

The Britt Diamond Ring

Every Diamond on the Britt team proudly wears the "Britt Diamond" ring. This ring is set with a round center diamond surrounded by six stones. We wear it with pride, and it symbolizes the fact that a Diamond IBO has achieved significance by helping at least six other people attain a degree of financial freedom through the business. Today, a new Diamond couple receives this ring for the man and a diamond pendant for the woman when they are first recognized on stage as Diamonds. This is a gift from BWW.

The symbolism of the Britt Diamond ring is of immense value to the IBO who has worked consistently to reach this level in the Amway business. When built the proper way, a Diamondship can provide significant economic security for most people. In that sense, many IBOs choose to quit their primary professions when they reach this level and enjoy the control over time and money that comes with it. More importantly, the Diamond level commands a great deal of respect and recognition. A Diamondship comes with annual trips to Hawaii, and exclusive trips to Peter Island, a beautiful getaway in the Caribbean. To a Britt Diamond, the ring is no less significant than a Super bowl ring to an NFL player. It signifies one's entry into an exclusive inner circle called the "Britt Backstage".

Prior to becoming a Diamond, Bobby Harris had been involved in high school and college athletics all his life. He had been exposed to "Good Locker Rooms" and "Bad Locker Rooms." He refers to the exclusive Diamond room backstage during BWW functions as the "Bill Britt Locker Room of Amway Diamonds," the ultimate locker room of men and women who value, above all else, honesty and integrity.

The Rocky Theme Song

Years ago, Bill Britt chose "Gonna Fly Now," the theme from the film "Rocky," as music for the recognition of a new Diamond on the Britt stage. To core Britt IBOs, this song represents achievement, financial freedom and an invitation to enter the exclusive Britt Diamond club. It is more than a great composition by Bill Conti. It has great emotional value to someone attending a Britt Free Enterprise Day celebration, aspiring to be a Diamond one day. My wife Anjali and I have been Diamonds since 1995, and have moved on to Executive Diamond and Founders Double Diamond levels since. But to this day, nothing gives us goose bumps the way the Rocky theme does. Many IBOs have even made the music their caller tune or ringtone, as a constant reminder of their goal in the Amway business. On stage, the only time this music is played is during Free Enterprise weekend, when a new Diamond is recognized for the very first time. It is often said that if you are unable to stop your tears from streaming down your face when this theme plays, you know you are going Diamond.

"Gonna Fly Now" represents the "pull" that the BWW leadership team creates for millions of people around the globe. It is the music around the battle cry for one's financial freedom. It is a beckoning to the upcoming IBO, signaling "If we can do it, so can you!" Reaching the Diamond level on the BWW team is of great significance. The Britt Diamond ring is symbolic and connotes that you've won the Super Bowl of life. The only difference is that unlike in football, the player gets to coach others as he or she moves on to higher and better levels. For many people, it is also symbolic of their freedom from a routine job.

If you talk to any growing IBO in the BWW system, they will tell you that their goal is to have their hands raised on BWW stage to the Rocky theme music by their mentors. The recognition event, called the "BWW Free Enterprise Weekend," is usually held at the Richmond coliseum in Virginia. It is the most elaborate and well-attended BWW event, and takes place during the fall every year. The 2010 event was especially significant. Bill and Peggy were not scheduled to attend due to Bill's ill health, and the special hand-raising ceremonies had to go on without them. Prakash and Smita Hegde were among the newly-qualified Diamonds. They were grateful that their immediate "uplines" were there to raise their hands, but they also felt the big void; this was going to be the first time in BWW history that Bill and Peggy were going to be absent from the FED stage. The weekend was otherwise exciting, and everything went well. On Sunday afternoon, as the event was winding down, suddenly, Bill and Peggy showed up. It was clear that Bill wasn't feeling well at all, but he still found the energy to go up on stage and raise the hands of each new Diamond to the Rocky theme. For those of us in the audience, it was one of the most emotional moments of our lives. There wasn't a single dry eye in the coliseum. As the Hegdes stood at the base of the steps leading to the stage, Ray Melillo whispered into their ears "You are probably the last new Diamonds whose hands he is going to raise." Ray was right.

The Greenbrier in West Virginia

My wife Anjali and I are from Mumbai, India. Coming to America brought us one step closer to our dreams of living a great life. Getting into Amway and becoming part of the BWW team was the real thing. It was the most significant decision of our lives so far as being able to realize the great American dream. One serendipity of surrounding ourselves with dreamers and thinkers like Bill Britt was that we were exposed to places and trips that we may otherwise have never known about or had access to. The Greenbrier resort in West Virginia is one such example.

The annual Britt Emerald Club was held at this place for many years in a row. (This was before it became a gambling destination.) For Anjali and me, this was our first exposure to a world-class resort. The property was lavish and the golf courses, magnificent. The dinner menu had no prices listed, and it was included in the cost of the room, which was certainly not cheap. One could order multiple entrees and indulge in what could be considered culinary heaven. The afternoon included "high tea" that came with a dress code. For many of us, this trip stretched our dreams and taught us about a whole new world.

I remember that during one of our trips to The Greenbrier, Bill Britt was in the lobby when we entered. He came up to me excitedly and said "Hey Kumar, have you ever seen the bunker?" I wasn't sure what he meant. This resort housed a 113,000 square foot bunker, built under one of its wings. This had been a top secret U.S. government relocation facility for Congress since 1961. Hotel guests had been blissfully unaware of its existence all along. But just that year, the Washington Post had exposed the bunker, and the government had declassified it. It was now open for tours. Anjali and I were just Emeralds then, but we did the tour with the Galas and the Britts. The most striking memory I have is how proud Bill was of America and everything it had done to protect its people and the idea of freedom around the world. He was beaming with joy, so much so that one might have thought that he had designed the bunker himself.

Since then, we have been to many places of similar or higher caliber.

However, for us, The Greenbrier remains symbolic of Bill Britt's ability to stretch our dreams and increase our self-esteem, and to let us know that nothing is beyond our reach if we remain consistent and steady in the pursuit of our goals.

BWW Charities

Bill would often talk about the importance of giving. In the Christian context, he would urge everyone to tithe 10% of their income. Many IBOs, including myself, started giving in one form or another after listening to his words. For those IBOs who wanted to give but did not have their own favorite charities, a great place to donate was during our religious services held on Sunday mornings during BWW weekend functions. Bill traditionally reserved Sunday mornings for church service during our weekend events. This was an optional event, and separate from the main session. While Christians attend their church service, the Hindus conduct their own prayer service, as do the Muslims, Sikhs, Jews and Zoroastrians. A few years ago, the BWW Management Operating Committee (MOC), decided to consolidate all the donations into a single entity, and BWW Charities was born.

BWW IBOs have certainly given away millions of dollars over the years for good causes, either through the optional religious services at major events, or through direct donations. IBOs regularly volunteer their time for charitable causes. Since its formation in August 2011 as a 501c3 organization, BWW Charities has donated and pledged over $1.25 million to worthwhile causes like Easter Seals and the U.S. Dream Academy.

Gracious Hosts

The preferred venue for MOC meetings is the Britt Estates in Florida. Bill and Peggy bought a beautiful home by the water in Ponte Vedra Beach, Florida. It was a dream home when they bought it. However, Bill was keen on making it a Dream World for IBOs and a meeting place for his top leaders. He had lavish additions made to the property, including flower beds, beautiful landscaping, a tennis court, a helipad and a fabulous meeting place atop his spacious garage that housed more than 15 of his luxury automobiles. The meeting place includes a spacious sitting area attached to a full kitchen well-stocked with snacks and energy drinks. A few steps above that are the Britt Walls of Fame, where he and Peggy have hung framed pictures of each of the Diamonds on their team. The pictures cover two walls leading into an elaborately designed meeting room, which is complete with the latest audio-video equipment, a huge mahogany table with intricate work, a vaulted ceiling and detailed paneling on the walls. Every addition was made keeping the IBOs in mind, so that when they visited they could expand their dreams and believe in great possibilities for themselves.

Bill had purchased several properties adjoining their abundant estate. Across the street he built a farm that housed goats, cows, chicken, ducks and pigs, and a vegetable farm that grew all kinds of organic vegetables and fruits.

Being hosted by the Britts is quite overwhelming. It is similar to being enveloped by a gentle hurricane of love, dreams and care. During visits, the MOC members would stay in rooms within the main house or in the farmhouse across the street. We would always try to go to a restaurant for breakfast in the mornings because we did not want to bother Peggy. However, more often than not, Bill and Peggy would insist, at least to those of us who stayed in the house, that we join them for breakfast. During the last couple of years, Peggy would make sure that Bill's meals were nutritious and wholesome, and there was always fresh, organic produce from their own farm. We treasured those times with them.

Years ago, at their home in Chapel Hill, North Carolina, even when the breakfast included sausages, potatoes, ham, cheese, eggs and bread, Peggy would make sure that there were enough vegetarian options for Kanti Gala. She would go out of her way to buy vegetarian sausages made of soy.

Executive Diamonds Manipal and Renuka Reddy remember their first invitation to the Britts' home in Chapel Hill. They recall how keen Bill was to learn about Indian culture and traditions. They were blown away to discover that Bill and Peggy had gone out of their way to order in Indian food, and had also taken the trouble to purchase some Indian music CDs for the evening.

Bill and Peggy would regularly host hundreds of people at a time. This required a lot of preparation and work, even though they had people helping them. But they never delegated the meet and greet to anyone else. They would personally (and Peggy does it to this day) reach out to every person who came.

Bill loved to share his homes, yachts and planes with the people in the business. We once had a chance to fly to Chicago in his newly acquired Falcon 50 for a meeting with Amway. He was really thrilled to show his plane off to us, and the underlying message was that any of us could own a jet like this if we kept building the business. Many Diamond IBOs have flown with Bill to attend different events sponsored by Amway, including a couple of concerts by Andrea Bocelli. Be it one of their luxurious homes, or his collection of cars, or an aircraft, Bill would take the time to show each visitor around and explain every feature, or tell a story that might be relevant, all in great detail.

Even if you were part of a group of a hundred people, each person would feel the love, care and attention of this wonderful couple. Come to think of it, this is not really much of an achievement for a couple that can make you feel special even when you are in a coliseum with 20,000 other people.

BWW Hall of Fame

Amway success stories seldom reach the world at large. They stay within the Amway family, shared through websites, functions and monthly magazines put out by the company to the IBO community. IBOs are some of the most passionate givers and are very involved within their own communities. In the true spirit of giving, IBOs seldom seek to bring attention to themselves or desire recognition for their service to society. A few years ago, Amway started to recognize IBO leaders for their outstanding work in the areas of Leadership, Generosity, Determination and Patriotism.

In December of 2013, the Amway Hero Award for Leadership was awarded to Bill and Peggy Britt. Peggy was honored at a special Achievers function in Miami, Florida, and presented the trophy, along with the recipients of the other three Hero Awards.

In 2011, the BWW MOC, under Bill's leadership, drew its inspiration from the Amway Hero awards and decided to implement its own "BWW Hall of Fame" to honor those who had spent most of their adult lives as unconditional BWW leaders and servers. We wanted Bill to be the first recipient of this award. Bill refused and insisted that other deserving leaders be honored first. The first three recipients were Diamonds Ray and Carroll Youngblood, Wayne and Carol Martin, and Executive Diamonds Al and Mary Anne Fratantuono. Ray Youngblood left for his heavenly abode in June of 2012. He was a great leader and a server, and will be remembered for his love for people and brilliant talks. Carroll continues to build the business today and carries on the legacy that Ray started. Wayne Martin was Bill's wingman in the early years. He and his wife stuck with Bill and Peggy through thick and thin. Al and Mary Anne met in college and spent most of their married lives building the Amway business. They exemplified a great "home team", and unconditionally spread their love to everyone in their sphere of influence.

During the BWW Free Enterprise Day function held in Richmond, Virginia, in October 2013, Bill and Peggy Britt were awarded the "BWW Hall of

Fame" award. Peggy accepted the gift on stage, and there was not a single dry eye in the coliseum that night.

In 2015, BWW inducted Executive Diamonds Rocky Covington and Ray and Joanne Melillo into the BWW Hall of Fame, and in 2016 BWW inducted Executive Diamonds Dave and Mia Taylor and Diamonds Runzie and Jean Valerio.

Chapter Captures

- Fame is not to be coveted. When one chases worthwhile dreams by serving others and following principles, fame chases them.

- Bill was a master dream builder. His intent was to create the pull, and teach others how to dream. He showed us possibilities and places we did not know existed. There are millions of people around the world who think about Bill Britt when the Rocky music theme plays, and not Sylvester Stallone.

- Bill always deflected all the glory and recognition he received to God. He never sought fame for himself. But when you serve so many people for so long, you become a brand.

Bill and Peggy host Kumar and his family on Bill's yacht.

Bill was always teaching, even onstage at a major event in 2011
with his Diamond leaders who are hanging on every word.

Peggy receiving the Hero Award for Leadership from Amway, presented to Bill and Peggy in November, 2013.

Bill & Peggy enjoy an outing at Niagara Falls during a break from an event.

Bill with his mother Vivian.

Influence and Inspiration

John Maxwell often says that leadership is influence. I will go one step further and say that leadership is inspiration. Even a hero needs someone to look up to and learn from. Bill's mother was the first hero in his life. Her determination and tenacity had a tremendous impact on him. Peggy Britt was his strength, and her dedication made it possible for him to reach his full potential. Rich DeVos and Jay Van Andel were his heroes in business and in life. Dexter Yager showed him an opportunity that totally changed his life.

Vivian Britt

Bill Britt adored his mother. His respect for her was immense. Because of his father's alcoholism, Vivian Britt had to become the head of the family, and was very influential in instilling some of the bedrock principles that helped Bill become the outstanding leader that he developed into. It is obvious that Bill got many of his character traits, like discipline and tenacity, from his mother.

Bill would often relate a particular incident from his childhood. He asked his mother if he could ride his tricycle. For whatever reason, she forbade him from doing so. Nevertheless, Bill went ahead and took his tricycle out for a ride. Soon after, Vivian gave him a whipping, using the World War I leather cap that he was wearing at the time. At first Bill remembers thinking "I can handle this." And then the metal buckle on the strap of the cap caught him in the butt and the back of his leg and he quickly changed his mind to "I can't handle this." Bill laughed about it, but he never forgot the incident. He would always conclude this story with "From that day on, my mother had my attention. She never had any problems from me after that incident."

A heartrending story that Bill would often share with us was when Vivian had been told that she had suffered nerve damage when she delivered her last child (Bill's youngest sister). Assuming that nothing could be done about it, she hobbled around with severe pain in her hip for 27 years. When her husband was unable to provide for the family, she took in boarders and cooked and cleaned for them, in addition to taking care of her own family. Bill was blown away by her endurance and will power. The irony was that she did not have to go through that much pain at all. The nerve damage had been a misdiagnosis. Almost three decades after the pain began a doctor discovered that her hip had simply been knocked out of its socket during childbirth. A titanium hip replacement surgery ended her pain.

A couple of days before Bill had been scheduled to speak to our team in New Jersey, Vivian passed away. We certainly would have understood if he had decided to cancel the event. But Bill came anyway. Bill did a great talk, and those of us who knew him well noted that he paused a couple of times as his thoughts drifted to his mother. Nevertheless, he gave one of his most memorable talks that night.

Peggy Britt

As I was writing this book, I was asked if there would be a separate chapter on Peggy Britt. Peggy's life was so meaningfully intertwined with Bill's that she is in every chapter. A book about Bill is also a book about Peggy. She is an exceptional example of someone who stood by her vows to support Bill in sickness and in health, in good times and bad, and in joy as well as sorrow.

A binary star system is one that consists of two stars orbiting their common center of mass. Bill and Peggy Britt's lives revolved around one another. Bill was the "primary" star and Peggy his "companion star." She preferred to stay in the background, but she was his real strength. Bill would often talk about the initial days, when they went through financial challenges. He would proudly share the fact that Peggy was just as calm and equanimous then as she was when they began to experience significant success and good times.

During their busiest years, Bill and Peggy have traveled countless miles to build their business and to serve people. Their work ethic was influenced by their love for the Amway business, their people and their faith.

Peggy has often been described as being "impeccable." Her demeanor, her clothes, her homes are always perfect. We have seen Bill and Peggy fuss at each other, but we have never seen Peggy lose her calm. That is just the way Peggy is. Anyone who is in her presence immediately feels her love, peace and warmth.

Rich and Jay

Rich DeVos and Jay Van Andel founded the Amway business in 1959. To say that they have influenced millions of people around the world would be an understatement. However, very few can claim to have had a close friendship with these two business giants. Bill Britt was among the few who could. The story of how Rich and Jay built their empire can qualify as a separate course in top business schools. It is a story that has made its appearance in many books on leadership and business. Many would argue that their work belongs in history books as being the essence of American entrepreneurship and the free enterprise system. As partners, they completed each other. Bill drew inspiration from Rich's ability to relate to people, and Jay's quiet strength, and their combined passion for God, country, family and the free enterprise system. Bill and Peggy seized every opportunity they were given to spend time with Rich and Jay and their wives.

Dexter Yager

Meeting Dexter Yager in 1970 was the turning point in Bill Britt's life. Bill often talked about how he had known he was in the presence of a master dreamer when he met him for the first time. Dex is one of the biggest dreamers the world has ever seen.

Bill respected Dexter as a dreamer and a leader, and recognized him as an authority in this business without question. They also shared a great friendship, and loved to laugh together. Dex often commented that Bill Britt was his best student. Together, they represent a sizable portion of the entire Amway business.

A few years ago, we surprised Bill Britt on his 80th birthday, right after our Free Enterprise fall conference. Many Diamonds and top officials from the Amway Corporation attended the event, but the real surprise was when Dexter and Birdie Yager walked in. It was a magical evening, the highlight of which was when Bill and Dex took the stage and reminisced about their times together in the business. They remembered the old days of brightly colored tuxedos and eagle belt buckles. They remembered how they would buy cars and motor homes together. They, along with their wives, had traveled the world together and really lived extraordinary lives. They mentored and led people to a better future, and they weathered many a storm together. Amway found some of its most loyal leaders in the Yagers and the Britts.

> *"Dexter told me and some others at Pebble Beach that there was no one like Bill. And then he went on for about 10 minutes on exactly why Bill was the best ever. When I told Bill about what Dexter said he just smiled and shook his head. 'No, Dex is the best. He's the Dream Giver.'"*
>
> *—Paul Miller*

Doug and Steve

The process of handing over the reins to the next generation of the DeVos and Van Andel families began many years ago. Rich DeVos underwent a heart transplant surgery in 1997. After a brave battle with Parkinson's disease, Jay Van Andel passed away in 2004. Rich is doing well, and is the longest-living recipient of a heart transplant at the time of writing this book. Like their siblings, both Doug DeVos and Steve Van Andel grew up in the Amway world. Most senior Amway IBO leaders like the Britts and Yagers knew them when they were little boys and have seen them grow and blossom through the years. Currently, Doug and Steve are President and Chairman of the Amway Corporation respectively.

As mentioned in the "Gratitude and Latitude" section, people who had a connection with Bill generously shared many stories and anecdotes. In most cases, I edited the content to suit the context, as well as for brevity. However, I have reproduced the following dialog between Doug and Steve verbatim. The duo took the time to sit down and talk from their hearts, to share their feelings about Bill and how he made an impression in their lives. They are both at the helm of a multi-billion-dollar enterprise, but their humility as they describe their appreciation for Bill Britt is noteworthy.

Doug:
I really can't remember the business without Bill Britt. One of the things about Bill that always stood out to me was the depth of his commitment. He was a force of nature;

larger than life with such a strong personality and strong beliefs. He believed in this business, in where he was going and where he could take others. He truly loved the Amway business and appreciated the opportunity it offered and he loved his group. That love and appreciation, that devotion, is a huge part of what made him such a success. Whenever there were problems or tough times, Bill never doubted and never lost his focus. He was dedicated to the business and his commitment never wavered.

Steve:

I'll always think of Bill and Peggy as family. When the business first began, when I was just a kid, it was all happening in the U.S. and with a relatively small group of people, very different than it is today. They were all in business together, all doing the same things all day long, spending a lot of time together and having a lot of fun. I remember the group getting together on a regular basis and they would be all over the house and you could tell that they were really good friends, that they were family.

Steve:

Bill did a great job of creating leaders. That was one of his greatest strengths. Not just helping people to build their businesses, but showing them how to do it themselves, and showing them how they could help other people. His business is still that way, filled with a tremendous amount of leaders that he developed, who have gone on to help others and are still strong today.

Doug:

Bill was known for saying the greatest leader was a servant leader and he really lived that. Whether it was his work with Easter Seals or his Amway business, he would just dive in and help other people. When he decided to do something, his passion and commitment would inspire everyone else to jump in too. He also did a great job of recognizing other people, putting other people on stage and in the spotlight. He really believed in helping other people succeed and that was his life's work.

Doug:

I remember a particular conversation that Bill and I had while traveling together about how leadership and life is all about decisions. The decisions you make in life, leadership and the business are so important, because if you make good decisions, you'll go the right way. So we talked a lot about how you get to a good decision, how you take the time to think through the problem and consider alternatives. He was really very thoughtful in his approach to the business and to life and I've thought about that conversation often.

Steve:

I've always thought that Bill was such a great example of leading and succeeding in all the different stages of the business. When you first start out in the business, you're busy growing and it's all about showing the plan, being in living rooms, introducing the business to others. Bill was a pioneer in this. Then it's about leadership and helping your leaders grow and working with them one on one, coaching and motivating. Bill was a master at this stage and developed so many other leaders. Then it's the ambassador stage of the business. Everyone looks up to you and respects you and asks you for your point of view and your support. Bill excelled at this stage too and through all of them, he never lost his passion or his commitment.

Doug:

One of my later memories of Bill was at an event in Orlando. I went up to his hotel room to visit with him, just prior to him going on stage to speak. He'd had a few health issues at this point and was moving a little slower. Peggy was helping him to get around and get dressed and I offered to help too. But the minute he got up on stage, everything changed and he just lit up. He moved all over the place, his energy was high—he was the great motivator we'd always known. I think this is just proof of his passion for the business, his love for his group and his commitment to helping them succeed. He believed so strongly in the purpose of what he was doing that it just overcame any little ailments or tiredness he was feeling.

Doug:

When I first started taking on responsibilities at the company in the late '80s, one of my first events was a Britt event in Richmond, Virginia. Maria and I were engaged so I brought her with me, and Bill and Peggy couldn't have been sweeter or friendlier to her. They made her feel so at home and so welcome. They even gave us our first wedding gift right on stage at the event. That was Bill and Peggy—welcoming, caring and generous.

Steve:

When Bill got into the business, free enterprise was a cause for him and Dad and Rich. Today we talk about entrepreneurship and small business ownership but back then, the words were free enterprise. And it was more than just words, it was a global dispute between capitalism and socialism. The business was founded on that idea of free enterprise -- owning your own business, controlling your life, being in charge of your financial situation. That is why Dad and Rich founded the business and that's why Bill joined them. Free enterprise was their cause and they fought for it and championed it, together. And look at what a legacy they created.

Chapter Captures

- Even heroes need heroes.

- Behind every successful man, there are people of influence.

- Bill's admiration and loyalty to the people who helped shape his success was unquestioned.

- The Amway business is multi-generational. Leaders like Bill Britt derived inspiration from the founding partners, whose sons, in turn, grew up observing and learning from these leaders as they were being groomed to take over the family business someday.

Bill with his first hero, his mother Vivian, and his brother Bobby.
As a young boy, Bill worked three jobs to earn
enough money to buy his mother a piano.

The Team:
The Power of Unity

Frank Luntz, the political pollster and a former consultant to the Amway Corporation, said this when he attended a recent BWW event: "I have never seen such a diverse group of individuals under one roof anywhere else." He was referring to the top leadership of BWW, which includes Asian Indians, Caucasians, African Americans, Chinese and other ethnicities. It includes a diversity of professions as well—we have medical doctors, PhDs, IT consultants, Nobel Prize nominees, engineers, politicians, musicians, mechanics, accountants, traditional business owners—you name it. Many of these people have achieved financial freedom through the business and have retired from their professions.

The leaders of BWW take pride in this spirit of unity and loyalty. We truly have a "one for all and all for one" attitude. It all stems from Bill Britt's fairness in the way he treated his people, in terms of respect, recognition and money matters. In terms of how the income from BWW is distributed to its various members, Bill Britt did not carve himself a special deal; he was subject to the same rules and regulations as all the other members are.

Masterstroke: Connecting with People

One reason for the unity in diversity was that Bill was a master at building relationships. He would always find a connection with people, young and old alike. One moment he would be challenging a teenager with a brainteaser, and the next, he would be sharing a story with an 80 year-old. He made kids giggle and adults laugh out loud. He always found a connection.

Raj Shah's marriage to Sangita had been arranged by their families. Bill discovered that Raj had interviewed a few hundred women before selecting Sangita. "Look at Raj," he would say, "he talked to all these women and the one he picked turned out to be the best. Here we have people carrying on for years and years before deciding to get married, and when they do, they also get divorced! Raj can teach Americans a thing or two about how to pick a bride." Later, Raj and Sangita built a mansion in Atlanta, which was a direct result of their building a large business. Bill admired Raj's persistence and vision, and teased him about his mansion. "Raj, if I continue to build the business hard, can I own a home like yours one day?"

When Bill learned that Diamond Nanda Sringari was a pilot, they developed a special connection. "We would share stories about flying, and Bill relished sharing his early flying days," recalls Nanda. "I have to say that they were all daring flights only a person like Bill would undertake. Interestingly, some of them involved Peggy when she was a reluctant but faithful passenger."

Diamonds Santhana and Ramaa Ramesh reminisce about their many memorable times with Bill Britt. Years ago, Bill saw the Rameshes' daughters perform Indian classical dance during a cruise trip with some of the BWW leaders and their families. He also learned that they were training to be figure skaters. After that, Bill would often inquire about the kids' progress, and would remember details along the way. On his 80th birthday, the girls performed a beautiful classical piece for Bill.

A few years before they reached the Diamond level, G.W. and Edna King spent a day with Bill and Peggy at their Chapel Hill home. Edna was fascinated with Peggy's garden, and G.W. with Bill's fancy cars. Bill invited him to sit in the driver's seat of his Rolls Royce and planted a seed: "G.W., you will own a Rolls Royce one day." That was G.W.'s hot button, and Bill knew it. After a period of hard work and persistence, the Kings ended up making this dream a reality.

Sugeet and Kaajal Ajmani, now Executive Diamonds, started out in the Amway business as accomplished professionals. The BWW Diamond team filled the void that corporate America had created in their lives. They were attracted to the values of godly principles and values espoused from the BWW stage. Sugeet yearned to be in Bill's inner circle. He and Kaajal were willing to do whatever it took to make that happen. Bill recognized this as they started to shine as upcoming leaders. This couple remembers when they were among a handful of people that Bill brought on stage from an audience of over 12,000. They remember how overwhelmed they were and even speechless. They remember the adrenalin rush that resulted from this unexpected gesture. Most of all, they remember how it increased their self-image when they realized that Bill Britt knew their names. The Ajmanis went on to build a large, thriving business that spans the globe.

Another leader that Bill had his eye on was Ganesh Shenoy, long before he reached his current level of Double Diamond. It was as if Bill knew what was going to happen. Ganesh did whatever it took, and showed the world what champions are made of. Despite many challenges, Ganesh's business continued to grow in multiple countries. Ganesh remembers Bill's words of encouragement and recognition, and most of all, his non-judgmental nature. Ganesh was a student when he started his business. Now he has a lifestyle that is admired by many.

In the business world, how often do we hear that someone attended a seminar or a convention that completely changed his or her life? With BWW events, this is a regular occurrence. When Bill spoke from stage, you either got mad or excited. In either case, he got you thinking. He opened up possibilities in your life that you had never known existed.

Executive Diamonds Tissa and Maithree Samaratunga talk about how the trajectory of their lives changed after they had listened to Bill for the first time, much like a moving ball on a pool table when hit by another ball. Tissa was in the midst of his PhD in Computer Engineering, aspiring only to excel in academics, when Bill planted the seed of financial freedom in him. This seed took fruit, and the couple now enjoys a great lifestyle through their business. More importantly, they appreciate the environment that comes with that freedom, one that encourages great health and family values.

Diamond IBOs Ajay and Alka Ohri remember their first few months in the business. Ajay was busy climbing the corporate ladder and wanted nothing to do with "the wife's" Amway business. Alka somehow managed to take him to a weekend function in Richmond, Virginia (it was his birthday gift to her). Ajay ended up staying in the hotel, catching up on his beauty sleep, and missed the Friday night and Saturday sessions. Thankfully he entered the coliseum toward the tail end of the Sunday session, when Bill was on stage, wrapping up the weekend. Ajay's life transformed in a few minutes, and the couple ended up building a Diamondship.

Bill recognized Ajay as a loyal, dedicated team player he could count on.

A strong reason for the tremendous unity in the BWW team is that its leaders have been teaching the same bedrock principles of team building for over four decades now. Years of experience have taught them to observe some boundaries that are best not crossed. Even though designed with the Amway business in mind, these are commonsense guidelines that can be applied to any organization.

Bill's 'Three Cardinal Rules' Principle

Any functional organization has a hierarchy. There are people above, below and sideways. In a traditional hierarchy, like corporations, governments and churches, the people "on top" are normally more influential and have a bigger income than the people "below" them. In the Amway business, that is not true. Someone "below" could develop a better-structured organization than someone "above." They could (and often do) have more influence and income. However, for the organization to function properly, there still has to be a leadership hierarchy, which, in the case of Amway and Britt Worldwide, is based on accomplishment rather than position. For the organization to function effectively, Bill came up with the following three Cardinal Rules that are the bedrock of the Britt Organization.

Cardinal Rule Number 1:
Don't do anything for the first time without checking with your mentor

I have heard it said that experience is the best teacher, provided it is someone else's experience. When there is lack of mentorship, people tend to make the same mistakes over and over again. By listening to someone who has gone before us, we can save ourselves from making costly mistakes. This could range from a new prospecting technique all the way to the purchase of a home.

The BWW system is all about mentorship. One serendipity while building a network of IBOs using the BWW system is the power of mentorship. During the Internet boom, I was tempted to join the frenzy of investment into new tech start-ups. When some of us ran the idea by Bill, he told us to be cautious. He also added that he was not going to touch those stocks with a ten-foot pole. For those who were listening, it was timely advice. Bill taught us to get out of debt and live well within our means. He often said that money should not take priority over relationships or peace at home. Bill Britt was the ultimate mentor; he went above and beyond, spending countless nights listening to others and giving them advice.

Sometimes, good mentorship means having unpleasant conversations to right someone's wrong, but Bill was a master. He mentored with love.

Cardinal Rule Number 2:
Never pass negative information to your own team or cross-groups

Problems and negative discussions should first go "up." If a leader passes negativity down to his group, he could demoralize them and shake up their confidence in the organization. Similarly, if people at the same level start discussing problems, it can become very counter-productive. They should first go to their leader. For example, an employee who is unable to resolve an issue should first go to his boss, rather than to his subordinates or someone else who reports to the same boss. In the context of our business, we encourage people to go "upline" with their pressing issues rather than "downline" or "crossline." In general, any organization with a hierarchy will do well to observe this cardinal rule. Bill would often point out that all functional organizations must have a hierarchy; be it the military or a private enterprise or even a family unit, the responsibility lies with the head of the organization to maintain harmony. At home, it serves the family best if parents keep their arguments private, and shield the rest of the family from issues and topics that are best not shared.

> *"When I come home after a hectic day, I don't dump all my problems on Peggy. Especially those that she cannot help me with. If I did, then I will have two sets of worries—one, the problems themselves, and two, the fact that Peggy would be worrying about them too!"*
> —*Bill Britt*

Cardinal Rule Number 3:
Never mess with anyone else's ego, money or spouse

Trust is the main pillar of unity. Showing disrespect to someone or publicly criticizing someone is one way to break trust.

Another way is to mess up with regard to money. In a corporation, it would be a disaster if the president decided to borrow money from all his vice presidents, and then do a business deal with the managers who report to the vice presidents.

Improper relationships or inappropriate behavior with someone else's spouse is the quickest way to break trust. Many politicians, businessmen, movie stars, CEOs and others have fallen prey to some form of infidelity. The recovery process is always long and arduous, and the damage often permanent.

It takes years of work to build teams based on trust and loyalty and only a few days to destroy it.

Many Britt leaders taught these rules over and over again. For the first three decades of its existence, it seemed like everyone followed the rules, and there were hardly any issues at the leadership level. Many people started to believe in Utopia. The belief that a Britt leader was beyond human fallacy was intoxicating and addictive. Most of the leaders who preached these rules started to believe in a standard of perfection that was, in reality, an illusion.

Testing Times: United We Stand

All this time, Bill would talk about being non-judgmental and practicing forgiveness. It was like he had a premonition, or maybe simply the good sense to recognize that humans were bound to err, and that he should prepare us for some corrections and aberrations.

Around the turn of the millennium, BWW faced some of its toughest times. A few of the top leaders went through divorces and some serious personal situations. Even though a divorce is a personal matter, the illusion of Utopia had led to seeing these leaders as "perfect" people who sat on a pedestal; how could someone with that kind of status go through a divorce? Bill and a few of the other leaders immediately went into their non-judgmental, forgiving mode. Bill pointed out that this was the time to love, not to blame. If there were any apologies or any corrections to be made, they would come later, not in the heat of the moment.

The Great Depression

It has been said that when it rains, it pours. A few months later, Bill himself went through some challenges—a bout of depression and anxiety. He was not himself for a while.

To be honest, no one on the Britt leadership team realized at first that something was amiss, with one exception. Claudia Nardone, who was familiar with the symptoms, saw the writing on the wall. She noticed the subtle signs that the rest of us missed. Looking back, it is apparent that Bill himself was confused and disoriented and unable to understand why he felt the way he did. He tried to mask it by staying busy and occupied. Those of us who were close to him eventually began to notice that he would periodically slip into temper tantrums and mood swings. He would talk about how he would sit in church and weep uncontrollably for no apparent reason. These sharing sessions were few and far between, and only conducted with his inner circle. To the world, he was still Bill Britt, the Superman.

Before he sought treatment and came back to normalcy, everyone, including Bill, was in denial. He continued to put up a brave front and do his magic on stage. The rest of us believed what we wanted to believe: Bill Britt was invincible.

A state of clinical depression does not develop overnight. It is often the result of accumulated experiences over long periods of time. Sitting backstage at a BWW function, Claudia Nardone reminded me that Bill's father's alcoholism may have had a much bigger impact on Bill than he himself realized. In Bill's own words, he lost his childhood years because he was too busy working to help his mother make ends meet. Having gone through and overcome depression herself, Claudia feels that having to be a bread winner at 11 years of age, and being denied the chance to be a normal kid, had to have taken its toll over the years. As I mentioned in an earlier chapter, Bill often joked about how his mother spanked him with his World War I pilot cap, and thus got his attention. Claudia wonders if his father's alcoholism and the environment at home caused Bill more damage than just that one incident.

Dr. Girish Desai, an accomplished doctor based in Long Island, New York, and currently a Diamond on the Britt team, looks back at the last decade of Bill's life. In hindsight, he can see how Bill's history of health challenges could also have contributed to his depression. Between the early 90s and the first decade of the millennium, Bill underwent a heart valve replacement, a bilateral carotid surgery, a bypass operation, a second valve replacement, and a split aorta. Kanti Gala connected Dr. Desai with Bill Britt.

Dr. Desai was very familiar with Bill's medical history and constantly urged him to eat healthy and stick to a workout schedule. Bill made several sincere attempts, but all those late nights, extensive travel and his love for food inevitably came in the way of his good intentions. Girish Desai observed that Bill's energy level began to drop, and his eating binges continued. These could very well have been symptoms of the onset of clinical depression.

The personal situations that some of the leaders were going through, compounded by Bill's erratic actions and emotions that came with his depression, caused reactions that ranged from panic to righteousness. The people who panicked went into a blame game. I went through some unsettling times myself, but ultimately I followed Kanti Gala's example and found myself somewhere in the middle of panic and righteousness, which was the place of loyalty and tolerance. I found my real teammates standing there with me. We gave Bill the love and support he needed at the time. We realized that our fearless leader who had taken on the world for decades was, after all, not invincible. Superman was now in his late seventies, and he needed some down time. He needed to be human.

When someone goes through depression, the people affected most are those closest to them. Peggy stood by her man like a rock. She helped him navigate the unsettling times. When all was said and done, Bill and Peggy emerged stronger, closer and more in love than ever.

Some people chose to part ways with BWW during that time. Those of us who remained loyal to Bill and the amazing system he created became stronger and more united than ever before. Today, BWW is recognized as being one of the leading organizations in Amway. We are better off now than we ever were.

You find out who your true friends are when you go through tough times. It is not always about who is right and who is wrong. It is about who your true friends are.

After a relatively brief period of quality medical treatment, Bill was able to overcome his depression. Other health challenges involving his heart and kidneys lingered, but mentally he was back to being Bill Britt, the Superman.

Home Team

Bill and Peggy and their leaders have always taught their people the importance of having a strong team in business as well as a strong team at home. Bill would point out that if someone had to spend all their energy fixing their marriage, they would not be able to effectively serve and give to others. Bill's own marriage with Peggy served as a primary example of his philosophy. Bill was a doer and an overachiever. Being his wife was not an easy task. Peggy made it look effortless, even though she had to work very hard to keep up with him. They both knew that they would be able to change more lives and give more to others if they were together in every aspect.

There was a period of a couple of decades when they had speaking engagements all over North America, punctuated by international trips, for 44 weekends out of the year. In addition to that, there was never a dull moment with Bill. He was always trying different diets and regimens (vegetarian one month, Atkins the next, followed by Dr. Fuhrman's diet and on and on), and Peggy had to keep up with all of that. She did, with a happy and humble heart. They loved each other very much.

At all levels, the leaders of BWW exemplify the Power of Unity. We now recognize that life is not perfect, and people are not perfect, but as long as we are united, we are a formidable, positive force.

> *"There are three kinds of people, those who can hurt, those who can help, and the ones that don't make a difference. To foster unity and growth, you should surround yourself with the people who can help you."*
>
> *—Bill Britt*

Chapter Captures

- It is no easy task to unite people from a wide range of ethnicities, religions, nationalities and languages. The BWW team is a great example of a true melting pot.

- It takes love, and sometimes tough love, to keep a vast team together.

- People need to feel empowered and free, but within boundaries. Unity is possible only when there are core principles and sensible rules to be followed.

- There is no dearth of fair-weather friends. The ones we can count on are the ones that stay with us during turbulent times.

- When people cross the boundaries, it is important to give them a second, or even a third chance before making judgments and sentencing them.

Bill Britt backstage at a business conference with Diamond leaders.
Bill's brother Bobby stands directly behind Bill.

Bill Britt at his home in North Carolina with (from left) Kanti Gala,
Raj Shah, Manipal Reddy and Shivaram Kumar.

Bill backstage with (from left) Kevin Bell, Noble Gibbens,
Paul Miller and Rocky Covington.

Bill onstage with Peggy at an event in the 1980s.

Bill was never more comfortable than when he was onstage in front of thousands of excited business owners, sharing his and Peggy's story of "overcoming to become."

Bill surrounded by leaders in the Diamond lounge in 2011.
Bill's ability to lead such a diverse organization—comprised of all races,
religions, professions and backgrounds—was unparalleled.

Mentorship:
The Power of Submission

The word "submission" often has a less than positive connotation. Many religions teach women to be submissive and "in submission" to their husbands. Bill Britt believed that every organization, be it a family unit or a huge conglomerate, has to have one head in order for it to be functional. It would be chaotic if there were multiple heads. He would also make it clear that the headship role is not an entitlement; it has to be earned. He would explain to us that a team can only submit to a leader if the leader first submits himself or herself to the team. His contention was that when done the right way, the one doing the submission has the power in the relationship. For example, when a student submits to a teacher, the teacher will be obligated to give his very best to the student. The student has the power, because he has surrendered his ego to and placed his trust in the teacher. The teacher has to be diligent in his advice, because he knows that the student is going to do what he tells him to do. The onus is on the teacher to see that his student succeeds. A rebellious student, on the other hand, has no power over his teacher. He cannot get the best from his teacher because he is not willing to receive.

Bill would often pick someone from the audience and ask them to give him a 20 or 100 dollar bill from their wallet. Then he would make a fist with the hand that was supposed to receive the money. The giver would try to thrust the money into the fist, but the bill would simply fall to the floor.

You cannot give to someone who is not willing to receive.

"I am not an expert at everything. No one is," Bill would say. "When I visit my cardiologist, I am in total submission to him. I pay careful attention to everything he says because he is the master on that subject. If you ever get pulled for speeding, it doesn't matter what your qualifications are, or how much your net worth may be, you must be humble and in total submission to the officer. To start with, he wears a badge over the left chest of his uniform. If that does not get your attention, you may look at the duty belt around his waist. You may notice that it carries a baton, or a taser, and handcuffs. If those do not convince you, I can guarantee you that his Glock 22 will."

Bill encouraged us to find a mentor in every important area of our lives. He urged us to be in submission to our mentor, to the rules and boundaries that he or she might recommend. He cautioned us against picking the wrong person for such an important role. "Make sure that they have the fruit on the tree," he would caution. "For example, don't follow my instructions on how to develop six pack abs, because I can barely reach my shoes to tie or untie them. But I do know a thing or two about creating financial security and leadership development. I know how to build a successful business. I know about people and relationships. No question about it."

Father Power

Bill Britt once delivered a talk entitled "Father Power." He talked about the importance of a father figure in one's life. This talk is a brilliant analogy between a family and an organization that one might be leading. It starts with Bill talking about his father, perhaps for the first time in public, from a point of view of understanding rather than regret. He admitted that when he was young, he would wish his alcoholic father was dead. Later, he realized that he might not be entirely to blame for his actions. The fact of the matter was that Bill's father had lost his own father when he was only five years old. Going one step further, Bill observed that his father's grandfather (his own great grandfather) had some inadequacies and showed a lack of understanding that had an adverse effect as well. In this epic talk, Bill asserts that as far as biological families go, what we each do affects four generations. Quoting Paul Miller and his son Johnny as an example, Bill explains that Paul is not just influencing Johnny, but up to four generations through Johnny, which could amount to a couple of hundred people. This is why it is important to treat people right and relate well to them. A father should never do anything that shames his family. When someone lacks in father power, then the offspring either follow the same pattern or fight their way out, learning from their father's inadequacies, like Bill did. Also, a father's role evolves as the child grows older. When a child reaches his or her teen years, it becomes important for a father to be a friend rather than a judge. Some fathers try to live vicariously through their kids, trying to make them do the things that they themselves wish they had done. They push their kids and become their judges. When a son loses a baseball game, the father should resist the temptation to correct and admonish. Instead, he should take him out for ice cream and have a talk. Mostly, he should encourage and empower. The father should assure him that win or lose, he is still his son and that he loves him unconditionally. Then he should encourage him to win the next time. This way, the son might actually come to him for advice on how to do better the next time around.

The Amway business allows one to build a network without limits. Just as in the case of Amy from an earlier chapter, when someone sponsors a new IBO, it starts a chain of sponsoring events that leads to multiple "generations" of IBOs coming into the organization. In the "Father Power" talk, Bill draws a parallel between these two relationships. He says that we are like parents to the new IBO. In the beginning, he or she doesn't have any idea how to build the business or what to do next. We take care of them and provide for them, like we would for an infant. As they start to grow and initiate other people into the business, we become like grandparents and great-grandparents. As they mature we must become more of a friend rather than an "upline." We must set the best possible example for them and maintain exemplary standards. Bill paints a vision for every member of the audience to build an organization of honest, hard-working, exceptional people who are kind, non-judgmental and a joy to the world.

"And that will make me, the great-great-great-grandfather, unbelievably happy, because I had a small role to play in influencing multiple generations of IBOs, just like a family," concludes Bill.

Bill used the term "Father Power" to explain to people the importance of the "headship" role in a family or an organization. He used his own childhood as an example of what it was like to grow up in a family without a proper role model, or to be part of an organization with weak leadership. In his case, he was able to turn things around and become the role model for others that he himself did not have growing up. The list of people who considered him their "Dad" is endless. In the IBO community, Bill's influence went far beyond the Amway business. People modeled their marriages, habits, words and principles on his teachings.

What was far less obvious was the level of mentorship Bill provided to people who had nothing to do with the Amway business. Every once in a while, we would get a glimpse of Bill helping a student from his neighborhood overcome a situation, and once even providing advice to a young entrepreneur trying to start her own "vegan chocolate" business. There is one incident that is particularly noteworthy. At Bill's funeral service, Double Diamond Lew Riggan noticed a couple of Hasidic Jews paying their final respects to the departed legend. Curious, he approached them, only to find out that they considered Bill their father-figure and mentor. These gentlemen did not belong to the IBO community and needless to say, did not belong to Bill's church. The details are not important, but, in what most would consider an unlikely gesture, Bill had reached out to them and made a difference to their lives.

Kanti Gala was just eight years old when his father passed away. Like Bill, he did not experience "Father Power" during his early years. Kanti felt an immediate connection with Bill. As Kanti and Lata moved up in the business and became part of Bill's inner circle, they became very close to Bill and Peggy. Bill became the father figure that Kanti had been looking for.

Kanti understood the meaning of submission. He submitted to Bill and his wisdom, and made him his mentor, philosopher and guide. In turn, he got the very best of Bill. Kanti became famous for his humility and stoicism. He never flaunts the fact that he and Lata have one of the largest Amway organizations ever built. He is not ostentatious, but if you look closely, you can see that he wears the best clothes and drives the finest cars. His appreciation of the good things in life is very tasteful, and not loud or boastful. His quiet nature fits well with the fact that he is a great listener and one of Bill's best students. He never stops learning.

I have had the privilege of having a wonderful relationship with Kanti. It was easy to have faith in Kanti because of his submission to Bill.

"People have faith in people who have faith in other people. People don't have faith in people who only have technical knowledge."
—Mark Diamond, Diamond IBO

My special friendship with Bill Britt would not have been possible if it were not for Kanti's inclusive style. He always encouraged me to spend time with Bill. He empowered me with a lot of responsibility and helped develop my leadership abilities. Bill recognized that I was eager to do more and he entrusted me with helping Kanti in different areas, especially the India market. As stated earlier, some of our most special moments with Bill were after meetings and early mornings at the Britts' Jacksonville and Chapel Hill residences. By observing Kanti work with Bill, I was able to understand the power of submission.

People learn about leadership, love, giving, tolerance and forgiveness from their mentors, among other things. But when the mentor goes through tough times, they themselves might not practice any of what they have learned over the years. The mentor may have forgiven his mentee and tolerated his or her imperfections, but the mentee might not be ready to do so when the time comes to return the favor. On that subject, Kanti remarks, "You don't put your father under a microscope. You don't abandon your father. No matter what, he is still your father." Kanti and Lata are fiercely loyal to Bill and Peggy, the BWW team and the Amway business. Now, they continue to treat Peggy like they would their own mothers. They are always there for her.

Executive Diamond Dave Taylor was playing left offensive tackle for the NFL Baltimore Colts when he met Bill (this was back before the team moved to Indianapolis). He had a good career, but he knew that he had to find something to do after football was over, and back then, professional athletes were not paid like they are today. This was all in the era of the Pittsburgh Steelers, Steel Curtain, and Mean Joe Green. The game often got nasty but Dave loved it, even though his body is still paying the price for it now.

Dave has fond memories of his own father, whom he loved very much. His father was not very outspoken, and Dave learned a lot of life lessons just by observing him. In contrast, Bill was very vocal about his views. This was a different kind of experience for Dave, something he felt had been missing in his life. At first, Dave had known Bill as a strong speaker from stage. As time passed, he was able to develop a personal friendship with him. Dave was drawn to Bill's sense of humor and his love for people. He recalls Bill's concern for the direction in which the country was heading. He remembers clearly when Bill referred to the ship called America and how many holes it had in its hull. Dave decided to join Bill in his mission to plug those holes and get America back on the right track. To Dave, Bill was like a dad, an older brother, and best friend wrapped into one. During his career from high school to the NFL, he had experienced some great coaches, but never one like Vince Lombardi, who, to this day, is considered the best to have ever coached the game. Dave had always wondered what it would have been like to play for him. Well, he found out: Bill Britt was the Vince Lombardi in his life.

Diamonds Sanjiv and Shauna Sahay, like many other leaders on the Britt team, refer to Bill as their father figure. The most significant lesson they learned from him was the one on vertical alignment—God, family and then business. This is one of the pillars of Bill's teachings. It conveys the message that chasing money by compromising on godly principles and relationships is destructive and counter-productive. Sanjiv became a vegetarian after listening to Bill's promotion of this lifestyle during a Britt event in the 90s. Even though Bill changed his mind soon after, Sanjiv laughs about the fact that he has never eaten meat since and is grateful to Bill for it.

Dr. Hal Newball has an impressive list of credentials. We like to say that he has more degrees than a thermometer. Prior to starting the Amway business, his nameplate read "HAROLD H. NEWBALL, MD, FACP, FCCP." While working as a professor at the Johns Hopkins Medical School, his expertise as a chest physician had made him famous. During the Cold War, the possibility of chemical attacks from Russia was a matter of grave concern. The United States Army Research Institute needed a new Chief for its Physiology division. Hal Newball accepted this important assignment. During the early 80s, he was one of a few handpicked scientists who were flown to Stockholm to make a presentation to the Nobel Prize panel. Who would have thought that a man with these many accolades would be subconsciously seeking some Father Power to guide him through life? His father had passed away in an accident before he was born, and it was not until he was under Bill's influence that he was able to fill that void. Now his credentials read "HAROLD H. NEWBALL, MD, FACP, FCCP, DIAMOND."

Bill's "Father Power" took root years earlier, and has evidently kicked off a chain of seemingly unstoppable events. In the business, it has affected multiple generations of IBOs in incredibly positive ways. Ray Melillo, now Executive Diamond, remembers how his mother Jean was upset and scared when his father passed away. As a young boy, Ray had to take over, and he did whatever it took to support the family. He shoveled snow, washed cars, and also started working the streets in the Bronx, building his "first network." This network, Ray contends, would have landed him in jail, but for the fact that he came under Bill's tutelage.

Ray ended up meeting Joanne through the business. Their entire married life, like Anjali's and mine, has been in the business. Their sons Joe, Nick, and Anthony are now building the business with passion. Jean, Ray's mother, and her second husband, Runzie (they married when Ray was 15 years old), were sponsored in Amway by Ray and Joanne, and went on to build a successful Diamondship themselves.

Similarly, Executive Diamonds Vinny and Dayna Pappalardo have been mentoring their son Tony and his wife Frances, and their daughter Danielle and her husband Dennis Nafte. Both couples are now financially free while still in their early 30's and have growing Diamond businesses.

In India, my father had always been an entrepreneur at heart, but did not have the opportunity or the mentorship to start his own business. That changed when Amway opened in India in 1998. At 72 years of age, my father started the business along with my mother. Both my sisters started at the same time. They have all built profitable businesses. Once, while greeting my parents backstage during a function, Bill said to me "In the business, you may be the Dad [referring to the fact that I had sponsored my parents into the business], but make no mistakes, in real life, he is still your dad!"

Lisa Madison, CEO of BWW, has been working for Bill and Peggy and BWW for over two decades. She is very proud of this. She is ever grateful that Bill gave her an opportunity and believed in her ability to be a part of the development of the organization and the preservation of the Britt legacy. This belief was certainly not misplaced. Under Lisa's leadership, BWW has made great strides in providing the most cost effective and efficient system that an IBO can hope for. Her relationship with the Britts is not a typical employer/employee one. To her, Bill was not only a boss and business mentor, he was a father figure and a dear friend.

She recalls, with pain, when she had to rush to South Carolina after her father suffered a heart attack while playing golf. She discovered that since no one had performed CPR, his brain had been without oxygen for 15 minutes, and he had slipped into a coma. The prognosis was not positive, and only the life support machines kept him alive. Unwilling to give up hope, Lisa started to look for options. She was keen on moving her dad to another hospital to get a second opinion. The problem was that the South Carolina doctors would not initiate the transfer. Knowing that Bill served on an advisory board at Duke Medical Hospital, she decided to reach out to him. It was a weekend, but Bill answered the call promptly, learned of the events that had transpired, and told her that he would call her back. Within 20 minutes, he called back. They had a conversation that Lisa will never forget. "Lisa, now here's the truth: your dad is probably already gone based on the situation, and he is in a better place right now, but I did speak to Dr. Cuffe [Duke's Chief Medical Officer] and he will be sending an airplane down to pick your dad up and fly him to Duke for a second opinion." Lisa fell to her knees and thanked God and Bill for giving her hope.

Of course, in the end, the Duke professionals agreed that Lisa's father's soul had probably passed two weeks earlier on the 13th hole of the golf course. She and her family had no choice but to authorize them to unplug the machines, and Lisa held his hand until his body passed. The outcome was the same, but thanks to Bill, her family had received the peace of mind and knowledge that they had made the right decision. For this and so many other things, Lisa is forever grateful and loyal to Bill and Peggy Britt.

People under Bill's influence had an insatiable appetite for his wisdom, common sense and practical advice. Though he had no children of his own, Bill had the experience of leading thousands of people, and based on that, was very qualified to offer parental advice. He would often remind fathers that their sons would learn from the example they set, and their daughters would pick a suitor based on their influence. He would caution people about the repercussions of a weak father figure. A father who expects his family to submit to him must first submit himself to the family and their needs.

"If you want to be treated like a king, make sure and treat your wife like a queen."

—Bill Britt

The Management Operating Committee

Paul Miller started out working at Peggy's warehouse for $3 an hour, years before he got into the Amway business. Paul had been an All Atlantic Coast Conference quarterback for the University of North Carolina football team, and earned a law degree following graduation. Paul never did practice law. Instead, the Millers ended up building one of the largest Amway teams in the history of the business.

Paul was loyal to Bill to a fault and for his part, Bill was proud of him. Paul credits his lifestyle, success, his belief, and his faith to Bill's tutelage. He remembers clearly the impact Bill had on his spiritual life. One day, after a meeting, Bill invited a few people to his house. Paul tagged along because he wanted to see the Britts' home, the place everyone was always raving about. When he got there, he found Bill surrounded by people, talking about the connection between the Bible and success. It had been almost a decade since Paul had been to church. But that night,

Bill read from the Book of Proverbs, asking people to stop him at any verse they wanted. When they did, he would connect that verse to a success principle. This event changed Paul's outlook on his spiritual life. Paul felt a special pull toward Bill Britt and his vision.

Paul is a true unifier. He and his wife Leslie are a blessing to the team. If there ever were a person who knew how to edify people, it would be Paul. Wherever he goes, he is constantly encouraging and uplifting everyone he comes across. You always feel like a million bucks and larger than life when you are around Paul. His wisdom and experience are crucial at our meetings where we make decisions that affect thousands of people. Paul is a master dream builder. He knows how to plant a vision and inspire millions to follow it.

Angelo Nardone was a therapist in the county school system when he was introduced to the Amway business. He worked with emotionally disturbed students from elementary to high school. He loved his profession but also realized that the income he was receiving with a master's degree in education would not provide for the lifestyle he wanted for his family. His wife, Claudia, was working for an Admiral in the Pentagon as an Executive Secretary. When Angelo started to associate with Britt leaders, he discovered that many men had "freed" their wives from working full-time jobs so they could raise their own children. Today, Angelo and Claudia have some nice material possessions, including a fleet of cars and motorcycles, but what really motivated Angelo in the formative years of his business was that he could make enough money that Claudia would not have to go to work. When they accomplished that dream, they set their eyes on their next big target, which was for Angelo to become free as well. They have been financially free for over 30 years. Today, they are among the most sought-after speakers in the world. They are a very humble couple, and have a huge number of Diamonds in North America, Turkey, China and many other places. Bill loved to kid around and laugh with Angelo. He called him the "skinny little guinea with ravioli eyes."

Angelo is synonymous with friendship, loyalty, energy and fun. Everything Angelo does, he does for the team. He has a sharp mind and stays on top of all the issues affecting Britt Worldwide. In addition to serving as an MOC member, he also heads up the Business Support Materials Committee. Ang works endless hours for the benefit of the big team. He is one of the best teachers and speakers that this business has ever produced. On the subject of unity, Ang often talks about The Lone Ranger. He points out that he was always alone except for one wingman, Tonto. The rest were called the Posse. Ang says that this business is a Posse business, not a Lone Ranger business. He loves motorcycles, and he organizes a trip once a year with his bike Posse from New Jersey to Britt Estates in Ponte Vedra Beach, Florida with a lot of exciting stops along the way. Bill looked forward to this event, as Peggy still does today.

Kanti Gala came to the U.S. from India in 1969 with $8 in his pocket. He completed his PhD in medicinal chemistry from St. John's University in New York, and was working as a scientist with a pharmaceutical company, making "good drugs," as he would put it. His wife, Lata, was working as an administrative director in nuclear medicine at a hospital. Having fulfilled the quintessential dream of having steady jobs and buying a home, it was no wonder that they started the Amway business rather reluctantly, Lata more so than Kanti. However, their first major BWW conference changed everything for them. That was 27 years ago. They listened to Bill and Peggy and their leaders, and were excited to discover that this organization stood for conservative values like respect for elders, strong marriages, family values and getting out of debt. Kanti also realized that his career as a scientist had peaked, and the path to moving into management was fraught with politics and glass ceilings. Within five years of that conference, Kanti and Lata had replaced their full-time incomes with their business income. Today, they lead a massive organization that spans the globe and enjoy a wonderful lifestyle.

Raj Shah migrated to the U.S. in 1982. Before he found a position in information technology at EDS in Detroit, he worked as a parking lot attendant. He and his wife Sangita were introduced to Amway by Sangita's parents. Skeptical at first, Raj transformed when he attended a Britt event in 1990. That is when they made the big decision to build the Amway business. At the time, they lived in a two-bedroom apartment in Troy, Michigan. Their strong work ethic and focus brought them steady results. On December 24, 1994, Raj retired from his job at EDS. He was only 34 years old. The retirement celebration included the Britt tradition of the smashing of an alarm clock, to signify that from that day on, he would set his own schedule rather than have a boss do it for him. The event was covered on "Eyewitness News" on a local TV channel. By then, the Shahs had moved into a nice single family home, and were debt-free. As their business continued to grow, they were able to move into a sprawling mansion near Atlanta, Georgia. Today they have growing teams in North America, India, the United Kingdom, Vietnam, and Australia.

I came to the U.S. to pursue my Master's degree in Computer Engineering. I secured a Teaching Assistantship that included a modest monthly stipend and full tuition fee waiver at Drexel University, without which my parents would not have been able to afford to send me abroad. As a graduate student, I did whatever it took to make a little extra money. I taught undergraduates and sang at Indian restaurants. My degree got me a job as a computer consultant with a company named Cap Gemini America. Once I got my green card, I started my own consulting business. I strayed into Amway because I was looking to buy health insurance through my business. At the time, New York Life had partnered with Amway to provide insurance for IBOs. My dreams and goals evolved from just needing health insurance, to making extra income, and to yearning for complete financial freedom. I started out single, and met my wife Anjali through the business (I registered Ajay and Alka Ohri, who are Diamonds, who registered Alka's sister, Anjali). Anjali and I got married in 1993. She was able to quit her job as a travel consultant with American Express within six months of the wedding. I retired from a traditional routine (9 to 5, doing computer consulting work) on June 17, 1994. Following the BWW tradition, I smashed my alarm clock outside the Bell Labs Red Hill facility in Holmdel, New Jersey. Thanks to our global Amway business and the Britt leadership team, Anjali and I have had an unusual lifestyle, filled with exciting trips and associations with remarkable people. Like Kanti and Raj, we have massive organizations in North America, India, the United Kingdom, Australia, and Singapore.

My first exposure to Bill Britt was in Lodi, New Jersey, where I met Verne, the stick man, for the very first time. I must admit I was skeptical at first, but I fell in love with Bill's style and his thought process. It took me nearly a year to really make the decision to build the Amway business. One major turning point happened on December 13, 1990. Bill and Peggy came to New Jersey to speak to Kanti and Lata's group, which was only about 200 strong in the Northeast area. I had a fledgling group of about ten people on my team. That night, Bill talked about the spoken word and shared his story one more time. He talked about the magic of written goals. Ever since, I have been a Britt student through and through. I have hung onto every one of Bill's words that I could. Anjali and I are ever grateful to Bill.

About a year before he passed on, we had the privilege of taking our three daughters to Bill and Peggy's Florida estate. We stayed in their farmhouse and enjoyed a guided tour conducted by the man himself, which included their mansion, farmhouse, farm animals and vegetable gardens, their condo, and a grand finale on their beautiful yacht. Our girls call the Britts "Uncle Bill" and "Aunt Peggy."

The BWW MOC has responsibility for the entire BWW organization. When Bill passed away, many people, mostly outside BWW, had legitimate concerns. What would happen to Britt Worldwide? Who would be the new head of the organization? Would anything change? What would happen to Bill's legacy? While these were all valid concerns, the truth was that Bill had already put things in place for this inevitable eventuality. As a matter of fact, due to his health, he had been unable to attend many events and meetings during his last few years. The MOC was put in a position to make many major decisions in his absence. While he was around, we always consulted him before implementing any of them. As it turned out, but for a couple of minor issues, he was in complete agreement with our recommendations. It became evident that Bill had trained his leaders well over the years. We also realized that even though none of us could actually be Bill Britt, we could think like him.

The BWW system transitioned into a post-Bill Britt era without any glitches. The MOC and the BWW LLC members work in harmony and continue to make decisions that benefit the multitude of IBOs in the system. CEO Lisa Madison and her staff execute those decisions in a timely and efficient manner. Every one of us on the MOC has been strongly influenced by Bill Britt's "Father Power" and we believe that the Britt legacy will prosper and thrive for generations to come. All is well.

Chapter Captures

- The Amway business is an intriguing one. Most people have no idea of the depth and breadth of this fascinating network. Built right, it can be one of the most rewarding experiences in relationship building and leadership development.

- The Amway business is multi-generational. Parents cannot wait for their children to get involved, and children often get their parents involved. They build legacies together. To dismiss the opportunity as a "scheme" or a "pyramid" is ludicrous.

- "Father Power" is universal. It would serve well for people in positions of leadership to understand this power.

- We always have to remember that whatever we do will affect multiple generations to come.

Bill loved the convenience and comfort of his Falcon 50 jet.
Bill and the Management Operating Committee before boarding
the jet (above) and during flight (below).

The MOC taking a break from a meeting at the BWW office
in Durham, North Carolina in 2015.

Management Operating Committee
members Paul & Leslie Miller.

Management Operating Committee
members Kanti & Lata Gala.

Management Operating Committee
members Angelo & Claudia Nardone.

Management Operating Committee
members Shivaram & Anjali Kumar.

Management Operating Committee
members Raj & Sangita Shah.

*His Lord said unto him, Well
done, thou good and faithful
servant, thou hast been faithful
over a few things, I will make you
a ruler over many things: enter
thou into the joy of thy Lord.*
                    —Matthew 25:21

Enter Bill Britt: Part II

At around 8 p.m. on January 22, 2013, I was in our New Jersey home when Kanti called me from Florida. He and Lata had just left the emergency room after spending some time with Bill. Peggy and Bill's brother, Bobby, had been present as well.

"Bill is on a ventilator," said Kanti, "but his breathing is steady, and we will visit him again tomorrow."

"Was he able to talk to you, Kanti?" I asked.

"No, he was not fully conscious, but Peggy was sure that he could hear what was being said," he replied. "And I was sure too, because when I was holding his hand as I was talking, he squeezed it a couple of times as if to say, Kanti, I can hear you, continue what you were reading."

"Reading?" I asked. "Kanti, what were you reading to him?"

Kanti reminded me that I had given him a couple of sheets of the earliest version of the chapter in this book entitled "Enter Bill Britt." In fact, those two pages were all that I had written at that point. I was completely taken aback when Kanti told me that he had read those pages to Bill. Tears welled up in my eyes. In my heart, I know that Bill had indeed heard those words from Kanti's mouth. That chapter is still my favorite part of this book, Enter Bill Britt.

"Kanti, I am sure he will be better tomorrow. Maybe I can just say hi. Please call me when you visit him tomorrow, and let me know when would be the best time for me to fly down."

Bill had been to the ER many times prior to this, but he had come out. He might not have been unscathed, and even a little weary, but he had made it through. The next morning, Kanti received a phone call. Bill was no more.

I was on the phone with Kanti when I walked into our kitchen. Anjali took one look at my face, and she knew. The world had lost a warrior, a champion who had dedicated his life to the betterment of others. Instantly, I was reminded of a story that I had once read about a 200-year old oak tree that had sheltered countless people and weathered many a storm and then fell suddenly one day, without warning.

A small ceremony for Bill was held at the Rouse funeral home in La Grange, North Carolina. La Grange has special significance for the Britt family. Bill would often talk about how he worked a whole summer for his grandfather for the grand fee of a quarter and a kitty cat! Bill had spent a good part of his childhood there, and his parents, grandparents, and other family members had been buried there as well.

Bobby Britt, one of Bill's seven siblings and a Diamond IBO in Amway, shared some wonderful stories about his relationship with Bill. Bobby was 17 years younger, and it wasn't until he eventually joined the Amway business that they had become close. He recalled that until he made his own mark as a Diamond in the business, he was known as "Bill Britt's brother." This did not irritate Bobby; instead, he was proud to be referred to in that fashion. Bill became his mentor and friend. He strived to earn Bill's respect.

Once, Bill gifted a pair of sunglasses to Bobby. Shortly thereafter, he was out in the ocean at Hilton Head, South Carolina, and a wave came up and knocked his sunglasses off his face, and he thought he would never see them again. A few minutes later, he felt something hit his leg. He reached down, and there were his sunglasses! Another time, he ran out of a plane to catch a connecting flight, and a flight attendant came running behind him with his sunglasses. A third time, he was unable to find them in his hotel room after a meeting the previous day. As he was leaving for the airport, someone came up to him and said, "We found these glasses by the pool. Are they yours?" Bobby pointed out that just like those sunglasses, we might think we have lost Bill, but we really haven't. "We know that physically he's not with us, and at times we may think we've lost him," said Bobby. "But he's always going to live in our hearts and our minds and our souls, and he's always just a thought away."

Bill is no more. Even today it feels strange to say that. As mentioned earlier, his larger-than-life presence, and the presence of his booming voice and piercing eyes from yesteryears on the videos at our conventions make us feel that he is with us each and every day. He is not "no more."

In fact, according to his faith, he has only moved elsewhere to be with his maker.

* * *

A jam-packed coliseum. It is not Richmond, Knoxville, Spokane, Shanghai, Chennai or Warsaw. This is not any time during the 70s, 80s, or 90s, or the first decade of the millennium. On earth it is January 23, 2013. But in reality, this is eternity.

We cannot imagine Bill Britt making anything but a grand entry, even into heaven.

It is time now. The stage lights are up. The music is unmistakable: "I Feel Good" by James Brown. Even here, everything is a little brighter and happier, if that were possible. The angels are celebrating more joyously than usual. The loud cheering in heaven's coliseum seems unstoppable, until Bill's Lord and Savior Jesus Christ takes stage. All of a sudden, there is pin-drop silence. Bill is waiting with bated breath to hear what he has been longing to hear all his life. And then the words come, resounding through eternity:

"Well done, my good and faithful servant!"

And the loud cheering and celebrations continue.
Enter Bill Britt. He is home now.

We can see Bill Britt playing the Gulbransen on stage with Vivian. Here he is, laughing and cheerful as he reunites with some of his closest friends, Ray Youngblood and Al Fratantuono. The next moment he is speaking on stage at a rally in heaven. We can see him in a nice car or a big beautiful yacht.

We cannot imagine him not being in charge of something, or suggesting improvements. Maybe he is suggesting a version of the "Rocky" music to the angels to add to their repertoire of songs to praise the Lord. He could be talking to God respectfully, asking him if he can give him some input on assigning guardian angels to his friends on earth. We can see him running into a politician, lawyer, or a Hollywood star that he did not approve of on earth, and then turning to Jesus, asking "What in heaven's name is this guy doing here?" We can picture him in active discussions regarding issues on earth, requesting special assignments for when the rapture occurs, and even making negotiations.

"My Lord," he might say, "I am a little concerned about my Hindu friends. They have no problems accepting You, but they also have a whole slew of other gods. They are good people, you know. Can we do something here? Maybe I can give you a list of people that I can personally vouch for…."

Like they must have said in heaven right before Bill's arrival, "You ain't seen nothin' yet!"

Bill & Peggy during a trip to Hawaii.

Billy Bernard Britt

August 28, 1931 – January 23, 2013

Homage

Every Britt leader has a favorite anecdote or experience that will remain with them forever. Sometimes it was Bill's humor, other times it was the message that humor contained. But every time, it was the genuine love and caring that shone through when Bill and Peggy interacted with people and gave of themselves unconditionally.

In preparation for this book, I sought comments, quotes and stories from the BWW leadership team. The response was overwhelming and extremely valuable. Needless to say, it was not feasible nor practical to include all of it in this book. Based on context and relevance, I have included many of the stories and comments in various chapters. This chapter is an additional collection of valuable input from accomplished BWW leaders.

"March 5th, 2011 will always be a very significant day in our lives. How could we not be excited? Bill and Peggy had agreed to meet and spend time with us. Bill and his loving dog Mustang Sally greeted us at the door. He told us that while he had just recovered from a viral infection, Peggy was still under the weather and would not be able to spend time with us. He, however, wanted us to say hello to her. Even as we meekly protested that she needed to rest, he took us straight to their bedroom and said, 'I have been married for too long. I know my wife. She would love to meet you.' We wished her a speedy recovery and then spent a most memorable afternoon with Bill. He showed us the whole estate; the transportation center with all his cars, the swimming pool, the veggie garden, the beautiful landscape and of course, all his animals. He took us to the clubhouse on his property. As we climbed the steps, it became very obvious that was a very difficult task for him. We tried our best to talk him out of it, but he knew what he wanted to do. Slowly, he made his way up and guided us to a special 'Wall of Fame' lined with pictures of Diamonds in identical frames. He proudly pointed to our picture and said, 'That is a nice picture.' We looked around, admiring the beautiful pictures of familiar faces and of the people who have been our heroes in this business. Bill's excitement was apparent in everything, whether it was the beautiful woodwork there and how he had managed to get the best wood at a great deal, or the lovely pond he had built, right across the street! His enthusiasm was infectious, his belief in the business and especially in people was apparent in everything he did and the way he lived his life. He firmly believed in our Crown Ambassadorship and tremendous success in the business. Our commitment is to prove him right."

Sugeet and Kaajal Ajmani, Executive Diamonds

"After four years at the United States Military Academy at West Point and five years in the Army's elite 82nd Airborne Division, I learned that not all leaders are the same. There is a rare breed of leader that people seem to be willing to do anything for. Bill was that kind of leader. The best leaders set a high standard for themselves first and then for others. Bill used to say 'leaders kick butt' then he would always follow very quickly with 'they kick their own butt first.' Bill spoke about God and country and the future. He answered questions with patience, as if he was hearing them for the first time, but we all knew that probably wasn't the case."

Kevin and Beth Bell, Diamonds

"One of my (Suzanne's) most memorable moments was during our first trip to Peter Island Resort, spending time will Bill and Peggy. Wayne had bought me a beautiful diamond ring in St. Thomas but it had to be sized so we were supposed to get it on our way back to the mainland. To my surprise Bill and Peggy brought it over for us. We were having dinner on the beach and when I lifted my napkin off the bread plate I saw my diamond ring.

"We once asked what would happen to all the material success after he left this earth. He always spoke about the earth being a temporary place and, knowing this, he planned to contribute to research that would help improve the world. He was a humanitarian in every sense of the word. His thought process and his vision for future generations were so far beyond what the average person thinks. Extraordinary is our word for him.

"Bill and Peggy are exceptional leaders. We are deeply grateful that we had the opportunity to know them, to listen and learn from their wisdom. The difference they have made is not because of their material success, but because of how they've shared their life."

Wayne and Suzanne Callender, Executive Diamonds

"My story exemplifies the financial freedom that the Amway business provides. Under the tutelage of Bill Britt and Kanti Gala, Pravin and I were able to build a very solid business. Pravin's passing had no negative financial implications to me and my family. Today my son Jinen and his wife are building their own business and helping me with my business, which they will eventually inherit, one day."

Madhu Chheda, Diamond

"The most powerful impact Bill had on me personally was that he motivated me to grow in every area of my life. Financial and business success came as I applied his teaching, but the growth spiritually, emotionally and developing myself in every area of my life over the last 36 years has been the most rewarding experience I have ever had with the most influential mentor I have ever met. The first time I ever heard Bill speak, he was teaching about the power of the spoken word and how you will live the way you speak. At FED 1978, Bill stood on stage and had the audience repeat after him words and sayings for 30 minutes, I had never seen a crowd so fired up.

"I have known Bill since 1977 and have heard him speak of Amway business leaders, ministers, military leaders and even ordinary people he learned lessons from. However, Rich DeVos, Jay Van Andel and Dexter Yager were always edified and spoken of as the most influential teachers and mentors in his life that I remember, especially Rich DeVos. Bill referred to Rich as his dad in the business."

Rocky Covington, Executive Diamond

"Bill taught us about 'Vertical Alignment'—God, Family, and then business, keeping God first in everything that we do, 'the power of the spoken word', serving others, and so much more. We attribute our success in business, and in life, to his teachings.

Kulin and Mina Desai, Diamonds

"The first time I heard Bill speak was at a function and he reminded me of an Air Force General. He spoke with tremendous authority, boldness and confidence. He was someone that you could just sit listen to all day. He was a man of incredible vision. From Bill I learned how powerful our words are and how you can simply speak your future into existence, and that everyone can be an architect of their own future with words they speak. Paul Miller once gave me a book entitled Don't Curse Your Crises and because of my crises I got to spend very precious time with Bill, during which he guided me through one of the most difficult times of my life. For that I'm forever grateful.

"We often hear that between the day you're born and the day you die, there is a dash that represents your life which will be defined and remembered by the people you've impacted and by the things you've accomplished. For Bill Britt that dash is a legacy that will impact and last for many generations all around the world in the most positive way."

Dave and Kim Doodnauth, Diamonds

"My strongest memory of Bill was the day I met him for the first time at a major convention in Virginia. I traveled from Brooklyn, NY at 27 years of age to learn how to be a successful business owner. I managed to get a front row seat in a coliseum of thousands of people. I heard so much from so many people about the positive impact this man, Bill Britt, has had in their life. The moment Bill stepped on the stage, it was as if each step pounded like thunder and his words vibrated my heart from his conviction. I was emotionally moved by his content later to find out his message titled 'The Why' became available on audio. I relive that moment in time every time I listen to that audio."

Charlie and Ann Durso, Executive Diamonds

"We were hosting Bill Britt at a Richmond function. I was so excited to have Bill in our car that morning and I took some wrong turns. After few minutes Bill said, 'TD, I think we are heading towards North Carolina.' I was so embarrassed and apologetic but it really didn't matter to him even though we were in rush. He just smilingly said 'Just wanted to make sure we could all attend the evening session' and we were all laughing. The mark of a true leader is never to make the follower feel uncomfortable or to put him or her on the spot even though he knows that they may have made a mistake."

Tirthankar and Suparna Dutta, Diamonds

"Bill and Peggy once came to Minot, North Dakota, to do a seminar. It was winter, about 80 degrees below zero. It was so cold the paint actually froze off the top of my car! Bill and Peggy both gave everything they had that night because they realized people had literally risked their lives to get to that event. I still remember how much Bill and Peggy wanted to make sure everyone got what they came for and more; how they just kept on loving on people into the early morning hours. It was almost 2 a.m. when Bill finally stopped talking, but people were still hungry for more so he sat on the edge of the stage and talked for another hour.

"On a lighter note, I remember how Bill loved to laugh and loved to have fun. He loved to tell jokes, but most of the time would start laughing before he got to the punch line. We've had water pistol fights, whoopee cushion episodes that almost got us kicked out of restaurants, and even a few things we probably should not talk about … all done in good, clean fun.

"The last thing Bill said to me and Toni when we saw him in the ICU at the hospital the day before he went home to Heaven was 'tell people about Jesus, tell people Jesus loves them.' And that's what I intend to do. Bill Britt was not only my business mentor, he was my spiritual mentor, and he was my friend and I miss him very much. I know he is rejoicing in Heaven with all his family and friends who have gone on before him, and I know he would like all of us to join him when our time on earth is over. God truly blessed Bill Britt and Bill Britt truly blessed the world."

Rick and Toni Fairchild, Diamonds

"We will fondly remember Bill for the rest of our lives. It would take days- even years to relate what Bill means to us. He was an uplifter, encourager, friend, teacher, mentor, and a great example. We wouldn't want to think where we would be if not for that divine connection that put Bill and Peggy in our lives. He left a legacy to millions whose lives he touched. Everything we know about success came from Bill's teachings and watching his remarkable ability to relate to all levels of people. Bill taught us how to think like winners and how to run like one. Bill empowered us to move on when we didn't know we could. Simply put, Bill created an environment where we could grow and we knew he would stand behind us. Bill knew God's divine purpose and he and Peggy stayed dedicated to their goals and dreams that included each and every one of us. They were like a mom and dad to us. We drew strength from them every time we listened to them."

Al and Mary Anne Fratantuono, Executive Diamonds

"There is a difference between learning success principles from a book in the 'Self Help' section at a bookstore, and sitting at the feet of a living legend. Bill's teachings are part of our everyday lives now. His contribution to our lives cannot be expressed in words. He inspired us to delve deeper into my religious books (we are Hindus), and I was grateful to discover that these principles are universal."

Sid and Rup Ganguly, Diamonds

"My connection with the White House started with the annual 'Washington Charity Dinner' on June 16, 1984 where President Ronald Reagan was Honorary Chairman, honoring his then Vice President, George Herbert Walker Bush.

"Bill's years in the military rising to Colonel, then City Manager, gave him great insight into how things really worked at many levels. Bill and I had many discussions over the years regarding President Reagan, wishing he was still at the helm!

"Doug Wead and Dexter Yager were Co-Chairmen of the Board along with such notables as Charlton Heston, Andy Williams, Efrem Zimbalist, Jr, George Kennedy, Billy Dee Williams and a handful of Diamonds, including myself. My role expanded with time, and I became a consultant with the 'World Alliance of Mayors' and then the Pentagon to assist in supporting their 'Warrior In Transition' initiative through our 501c3, non-profit, The Hope Collection, named after my mother Hope!

"Bill's wisdom, dispensed though endless conversations as we hosted them at functions and excursions to their homes and on their boats,were very helpful as I carried out my responsibilities as a consultant."

Joel & Ardith Griffing, Diamonds

"Having coached high school basketball and baseball for 15 years by 1977, I thought I knew through my association with other coaches what real men were like. The fact was, apparently I didn't even know if I was a real man. I first met Bill Britt in late August 1977 after becoming an independent business owner in Amway – as a 'why not' thought process. In a meeting in Arlington, Virginia, I became exposed to a thought process I had never heard of. That night Bill talked about, among other things, the power of the spoken word. That what you say is what you get, that you are snared by the words of your mouth. That your tongue is your creative force. The next month, September, in Charlotte, North Carolina, Bill talked about the free enterprise system and how it relates to our country's past and future. The next month, October, at a Sunday morning non-denominational church service in Hazelton, Pennsylvania, Bill was the conduit for my acceptance of Jesus Christ as my personal Lord and Savior. As a result of that, I was given a foundation on which to build my future. Thankfully, by changing my foundational thought process, I could begin to change my family's future and then my grandchildren's future."

Bobby and Priscilla Harris, Diamonds

"When I was a young man, it was Bill's beliefs, convictions and his unique way of expressing them that had a major influence of my business career. I never tired of listening to him and any success I have enjoyed in life can be attributed to the influence of Bill. One of my greatest honors is that Bill became a good friend. He was and will always remain a lifelong mentor. I was privileged to have known him and will spend the rest of my life passing on the lessons he taught me. The world is a much better place because he lived."

Bill Hawkins, Executive Diamond

"Bill Britt's 'handle' in the old days was 'The Lamplighter' because he lit the way for us with a relentless passion and belief. He was tenacious, compassionate and caring. We love and miss you, Big Daddy!"

Brian Herosian, Executive Diamond

"Bill Britt always came across as a strong personality, but it was more of him being strong on principles and gentle on people. He taught us about the basics of success like the law of sowing and reaping. Bill Britt said that you cannot have any type of freedom unless you are economically free. He taught us that the measure of true success is how many people are better off because you lived. Personally for us, Bill Britt became a standard of success. By following his teachings we were confident that we would be financially successful. He taught us what we would not have learned otherwise. Bill emphasized the importance of reading and because of him reading has become more of a habit, which has trickled down to our kids' reading every night."

Vishal and Sonika Jain, Diamonds

"People often ask us, 'What is your most profound memory of Bill Britt?' Many think it must be of having our hands raised on stage at FED or flying on his jet to hear Andrea Bocelli perform or spending the day with him and Peggy on one of their yachts. Those all pale in comparison to going to church with them on a quiet Sunday morning in Florida, sitting in the pew and hearing the message for the day and looking over and seeing Bill hold Peggy's hand. Being at perfect peace with himself and the world and so in love with his wife. That is without a doubt our very best memory of the man and legend, Bill Britt."

Tom and Estelle Joachim, Diamonds

"Bill Britt is my friend, mentor, coach and leader in every area of my life. His influences and examples have a large part in the person I am today. There are countless highlights of the times I have spent with Bill. I first spoke with Bill when he and Peggy spoke at a Seminar in Dallas, Texas, February 1978. He invited me to the Sunday Leadership meeting and I told him I did not qualify. He said 'Don't worry about that and tell the host I told you to come.' I went and caught some of his vision and a larger picture of this business. A few months later, he was speaking at an attitude session in Virginia. I asked my sponsor, David, if I could attend. Bill heard that I flew there from Texas for the meeting and said that I was either crazy or I was going Diamond. On several occasions Bill would ride my sons Markus, Kevin and David on his back in swimming pools, race them across tennis courts, he would sit and talk with them. He accepted my family and me. Other special moments: driving him and Peggy in their limo, flying with them in their private airplane, riding in their motor coach, being a guest in their home and having deep conversations about things that really make a difference in this world. He added value to my life. He poured so much of his life into so many; his legacy will live for a long time."

Marshall Johnson, Diamond

"Each time we were around Bill, we wouldn't want him to stop talking. We cherished his words and his wisdom. A single thought or advice from Bill could change someone's life for the better. We promise to carry on his legacy and continue to share his message of love."

Rashmiranjan and Smita Jyotiprakash, Executive Diamonds

"For us, Bill Britt was truly larger than life; a hero, a father figure, and a culture warrior. He exemplified passion, dedication, focus, integrity, and objectivity. We will always remember not only Bill Britt—the leader of people; but also, Bill Britt—the person behind the stage. Our last moments with Bill were after he was no longer there physically. As we held his hand for the last time standing by his coffin, on the day of the viewing, we remember that he looked so majestic in death—as in life. On his coffin were three buttons: 'The Lord is my Shepherd', 'Honor and Courage', 'Let my work speak for me'—how fit for a warrior like Bill!"

Chak and Uma Kakani, Executive Diamonds

"I was fortunate to meet Bill Britt shortly after starting my Amway business. My first impression was that he was a man of God. We had reached the Emerald level in Amway, which means helping three IBO-ships reach the Platinum level. I was banking my civil engineering checks. I asked Bill whether I should quit my job. Bill looked at my business organization and advised me to keep working until I hit the Diamond level in Amway, which means helping six IBO-ships reach the Platinum level. He said, 'You are close to it now; just keep showing the business plan at the same rate.' Then Bill continued: 'When you go Diamond, we will have a very special freedom banquet in your honor. We will use the Washington Hilton ballroom and have more than 2,000 people come to celebrate your financial freedom. It will be a black-tie affair, and we will have a Rolls Royce to pick you and your family up. It will be an event that the people in Washington DC, will never forget.' With those words, Bill built my dream. A year later, Edna and I were qualified Diamond and the dream came true. Our freedom banquet was at the Washington Hilton ballroom on August 20, 1981, with more than 2,000 people in attendance. Bill and Peggy were our guest speakers. The event was phenomenal. A year later I purchased my own Rolls Royce, because Bill inspired me to believe in my dream."

G.W. and Edna King, Diamonds

"Bill particularly enjoyed the topics of money, politics and, of course, religion. Sometimes it was hard and we wanted to debate with him on so many points but, somewhere inside, we knew he was right about most, if not all, of them. We'd argue with him but not directly, just quietly within our own minds, or once in a while with each other. And like most times when finding something we may not have liked to hear, it only wasted time and energy which would have been better spent building our lives and businesses instead.

"It was a fun and exciting to be schooled by this extraordinary man. Our first spiritual encounter with Bill came when we attended a Sunday non-denominational Christian service. We received that morning what would become the beginning of the most amazing spiritual journeys of our lives. Thanks for the memories, Bill. Whether dancing until your necktie was soaked or downing almost a dozen cannolis backstage at a seminar, or eating hot sauce-soaked food until sweat poured down your face while hanging in Little Italy...thanks! Thanks for always making this business as serious as a heart attack and yet, more fun than anything else we could ever think to do with our lives! You were like a father to a fatherless boy, who you helped groom into a man...and become a father to many. Finally, even though you were not as well in recent years, you tirelessly poured into our sons while walking around your property during an impromptu visit. You instilled an even greater vision in them as you loved on them that day as though they were your very own. It was a day they shall never forget."

Ray and Joanne Melillo, Executive Diamonds

"I was Bill's friend for 38 years. My father was happy that I had this friendship and mentorship and spiritual leadership in my life. I truly and sincerely thank God for Bill Britt. Many top Amway leaders not in Bill's group have asked me what it's like to be around Bill. They would see and hear Bill on stage where he didn't mince words about right versus wrong, Hollywood, Castro, liberals, our military, the Constitution, abortion, high taxes, men vs. wimps, hard work...

"Off the stage, Bill Britt is mainly a teddy bear who loves to laugh and kid around. God gave Bill the gifts of exhortation and discernment. He was always excited to see you and encourage you and he knew when you were hurting and why. If Bill offended someone, he was quick to apologize. Honesty and loyalty were not just words to be spoken from stage; he lived them. But to me, the greatest characterization of Bill was 'Forgiveness.' He often said there was only one perfect person in all of humanity. Bill explained most people who were 'Judges' may not have been doing what the person they were judging was doing, but they were doing five things they could be judged on.

"Bill loved what he learned from serving his country under combat conditions in Korea. He once almost tossed a U.S. politician off Amway's yacht when the politician said the Constitution was 'just a piece of paper.' Later, this 'famous and powerful' politician was forced out of Congress for an ethics violation.

"Bill was at the airport newsstand once and spotted a well-dressed businessman looking at a 'girlie' magazine. Bill quietly told the man 'You're better than that.' Red-faced, the man put the magazine back on the rack and walked away.

"In 1975, Bill gave a very interesting talk which I didn't understand at the time. Working as a City Manager, while getting his Master's degree, he noticed the work ethic of 'most' government employees, and he began talking about 'laying sideways in the public trough.' He warned that America would be doomed if half the citizens began to look to the government for a check.

"When I went through my toughest trial ever, Bill Britt was there.... My dad had passed away and Bill stepped in. When people turned on me and judged me, Bill never wavered in his friendship. In good times and bad times, a true friend."

Paul and Leslie Miller, Crowns

"Without Bill being the strong leader he was, my family would never have been able to get out of a tumultuous financial situation. We will forever miss his grand entrances on stage, dancing away with such wonderful rhythm."

Dennis and Danielle Nafte, Diamonds

"The Britt legacy will never fade. We will work diligently to pass it on to future generations."

Tony and Frances Pappalardo, Executive Diamonds

"We are all products of our environment, in my case it was a limiting middle class upbringing. Bill taught us to dream, to boldly speak those dreams and pursue them with passion. He helped us understand that we are designed to overcome challenges and become. That life is not a zero-sum game and that true success is how many people are better off because you lived. Bill lived these teachings. He overcame adverse situations throughout his life and in so doing, his life was a message for us. Bill spent his lifetime building people up. While tough on stage he had this incredible endearing touch. We were new Emeralds assigned to host Bill and Peggy. In fact, we had just gotten a used Cadillac, our first luxury car. As someone who had owned hundreds of luxury cars throughout his lifetime, this was just another car, and not such a great one. But for Bill, it was one more opportunity to make an up and coming leader feel special. He must have spent a good 15 minutes looking it over and complimenting us!"

Chetan and Vineeta Rastogi, Diamonds

"We traveled from Toronto to Virginia Beach for our first Winter Conference. We were excited to be able to see Bill and Peggy for the first time. Our hope was to just get a glimpse. To our utter amazement, Bill walked up to our group and started dancing with us during the music break. He was a legend, but he was also down to earth and did not have any airs about him."

Firdosh and Nilofer Sethna, Diamonds

"Bill Britt made an incredible impact in our lives when he said, 'You are the first Russian couple in BWW making it big in the business, and I'd like to bless and pray over you, so God will bless your efforts.' He prayed, he blessed us...and for us this was such a historical moment in our business, that such a legend was praying to God for his blessing over us. We love and miss him dearly, but we will carry his torch for him, along with the hundreds of others who were just as impacted as we were."

Valeriy and Nadia Solodyankin, Diamonds

"Bill spoke about God, Country, Family and Freedom which electrified us and woke up the sleeping giant within us. That first exposure to Bill Britt made all the difference to us because he spoke about who we were, where we came from and that we were created for a purpose; he hit all the right chords to spring us into action. He has impacted us through the teachings of Three Powers, Written Goals, Golden Rule, Honesty and Integrity, self-image and attitude. Our kids, parents and everyone around us know these powers that unlock the key to success.

"Until I met Bill, I used to think in terms of short and long range goals but never imagined that a person can have goals for his LIFE and that goals should be big enough that you reach your goals beyond your lifetime! That taught me that I can achieve something magnificent out of my life, gave meaning and perspective to my life, have God use my life for a greater purpose. As I live a purpose driven life I will always have this perspective. Bill's goal of breaking 100 diamonds a year in North America was one such goal. We will be a big part of that."

Nanda and Sangeetha Sringari, Diamonds

"I remember Bill's handshake; it was a man's handshake and I could feel his strength. He looked me straight in the eye with a big smile and treated me like he had known me for a long time. I immediately liked him; little did I know that he was going to change my life in so many ways.

"Any time we had functions or conferences, my best buddy Brian Herosian (an EDC and former NFL and CFL star), and I would always be the last people to see Bill before he would turn in for the night. Can't count the times we would get one last nugget just before he went into his room. Just one nugget would keep me and Brian talking for hours. He had that kind of wisdom and understanding on countless subjects.

"We believed in Bill, we trusted Bill, we couldn't wait to see him again. He loved people and it showed. I never saw him give a talk from notes; it always came straight from his heart. He had this great ability to know what people needed to hear. Bill being the spiritual person that he was, he would just say a prayer and ask God to speak through him, and it felt like He always did.

"Bill was a Man's Man. You could talk to him about anything, he wouldn't judge you, and he would just help you get back on the right track again. One of my greatest desires was for Bill to know me and to be proud of me. He was just that type of person, that type of coach. You wanted to win for him. Bill taught me to think big, love people, fight for what was right and to give God all the credit. He taught me how to be a problem solver instead of giving up and quitting. He taught me patience and to know that everything was in God's timing. He taught us that believing in people was one of our most important powers that we have as human beings. The most important thing I learned from Bill was that God loved me and that he had big plans for my life."

David and Mia Taylor, Executive Diamonds

Bill and Peggy set the example for how to enjoy a full life together, both in quiet moments and in a coliseum filled with devoted and enthusiastic business owners.

Bill Britt as a young Army officer during the Korean War (above),
and as the leader of over 1.5 million business owners.

Bill during a trip to the Holy Land in the 1990s (above)
and dancing with Peggy at a surprise 75th birthday party in 2008.

Bill and Peggy in Greece during a Mediterranean cruise aboard the Amway Enterprise V yacht.

Iron Man, Silken Heart

Iron Man, Silken Heart